RFID

Strategic Implementation and ROI

A Practical Roadmap to Success

CHARLES POIRIER • DUNCAN McCOLLUM

ISBN 1-932159-47-9

Printed and bound in the U.S.A. Printed on acid-free paper
10 9 8 7 6 5 4 3 2 1

Library of Congress Cataloging-in-Publication Data

Poirier, Charles C., 1936-
   RFID strategic implementation and ROI : a practical roadmap to
success / by Charles C. Poirier & Duncan McCollum.
      p. cm.
   Includes bibliographical references and index.
   ISBN 1-932159-47-9 (hardback : alk. paper)
   1. Radio frequency identification systems—Technological innovations
—Economic aspects. 2. Business logistics—Technological innovations.
   I. McCollum, Duncan, 1957-. II. Title.
   HD38.5.P6377 2005
   658.7'87—dc22   2005022254

Phone: (954) 727-9333
Fax: (561) 892-0700
Web: www.jrosspub.com

DEDICATION

For my family
—*Chuck*

To Laura, for your never-wavering belief and support.
For Skylar, Cooper, Mackenzie, Duncan, and Brittany
for always reminding me what is really important.
—*Duncan*

CONTENTS

PREFACE

From time to time, new technologies appear amid much fanfare regarding the impact they will have on business and society. Some are quickly accepted, others move through a slow but relentless adoption curve, while still others are rejected. Wireless technology was originally viewed by the telecoms as a temporary nuisance, but has moved on to spawn a multibillion-dollar industry. The transistor and personal computer went through a slow but inevitable adoption cycle. When the jet engine was introduced to the military, it went through a similar growth cycle. Conversely, the effect that penicillin had on medicine and health care was rapid and fortuitous.

SPEED AND ACCEPTANCE

In the terms of Charles Fine, professor at MIT and author of the book *Clockspeed,* a new technology can progress through one of two scenarios. It can exhibit innovative dynamics and transition through a series of slow adoption and performance cycles, or it can move through a much more rapid and greater series of cycles. The drive for internal combustion engine fuel economy and the current effort to introduce fuel cells in cars represent the slower clockspeed cycles, possibly requiring decades for full acceptance. Mass production, the Dell direct operating model, and lean manufacturing are examples of the faster and more radical cycles. In an endless cycle of such introductions, each innovation has its advocates and cynics. The mini steel mill was greeted with derision by the established manufacturers, much to their regret. Air-conditioning and elevators met with rapid acceptance.

And now we have radio frequency identification (RFID). Proponents insist this technology will be disruptive and move through a very rapid acceptance and implementation cycle. They point to the considerable media coverage and examples of early adoption. Mark Roberti, founder and editor of the *RFID Journal,* claims for the advocates that "RFID will affect every large and mid-size company that makes, transports, or sells products — in every industry" (Roberti 2005a). Opponents insist it is no more than a temporary phenomenon and an extension of already accepted and applied systems. This cynical camp holds out the Universal Product Code (UPC) and bar coding as the prevailing standard and system. Somewhere in the middle is a host of observers with a wait-and-see attitude, trying to sort through advocacy and opposition. These watchers seek direction and long for documentation of the actual costs and benefits.

From a business sense, there are a host of questions to be answered, including: What are the real costs and benefits? What's in it for my company? How fast should our firm move? How much risk is involved? As practitioners, researchers, and authors, we stand on the side that counsels RFID is an unstoppable technological introduction, and eventually all companies pursuing supply chain optimization will need to apply the concepts as an integral part of the drive for cost control, visibility, and manufacturing and delivery efficiency across extended enterprises. Regardless of your position, RFID is already becoming a part of your life — as you drive through tollbooths, open keyless automobiles, and use plastic cards for building access identification. It is on your horizon, and effective strategies regarding its use need to be developed to take greatest advantage of the possible benefits. RFID is destined to be a disruptive technology that will have a slow start-up ramp, followed by rapid clockspeed acceptance and a relentless series of documented improvement stories. It will be a technology that will find its way into a rash of applications, industries, and individual businesses, undoubtedly impacting our professional and personal lives.

CONTROVERSY AND RESOLUTION

RFID technology and its adoption and deployment path will encounter challenges and face another series of tactical questions. What is the right tag cost? What is the optimum hardware configuration? What data should be captured and how should the data be managed? How will RFID affect our legacy and enterprise resource planning (ERP) systems? How can the concepts be effectively applied across today's complicated interorganizational supply chain networks? We do not propose a single answer to these questions or a simple solution, since we realize that each impacted business environment will be different. Rather, a degree of customization will be necessary for consumer goods, transportation and delivery systems, retail operations, military resources, personal applications, and so forth. There already has been too much hype around "RFID-in-a-box" quick-hit type of solutions or "slap-and-ship" easy applications. Those ideas will ultimately be surpassed because they are full of vague promise of immediate compliance without the provision of ultimate benefit and return on investment.

For those dedicated to business applications and achieving supply chain optimization, there is yet another question: How does RFID fit with or support your supply chain strategy? Our position here is also clear. RFID will end up being one important part of another relentless drive — for total visibility across a supply chain network. The real goal of supply chain management is to use the fruits of such an effort not just to reduce costs and become more flexible and responsive, but to better satisfy key customers and build new revenues. To accomplish both purposes, there is a need to have visibility into the end-to-end processing that takes place across an extended enterprise. Such visibility can only be enhanced with the use of RFID technology.

RFID becomes a tool for helping visibility, but that feature does not stand alone as a defining characteristic. The ultimate value of RFID is the knowledge it provides, which must be integrated with other valuable information in cross-business communication systems. Practitioners want to know not just where their products might be but how that knowledge can be used — to be more effective in their business processing and eventually to sell more product. The real benefit will come when RFID is integrated as part of a drive for supply chain optimization, full network connectivity, and ERP-to-ERP communication that tells the business partners what the supply might be, where it is, and how it can be brought to the point of need, in quantities that match the actual demand. When it also helps in the data analysis that leads to generating new revenues, the cake will be iced.

THE PROMISES AND PROBLEMS

Often called by advocates the "next big thing in business," RFID is currently one of the most talked about emerging technologies. But is it a temporary nuisance or an unstoppable business improvement process? On the one hand, RFID promises full supply chain visibility and a means to transfer complete product data across an end-to-end business network. From farms to dinner tables, the chance is now present to tag animals before slaughter and follow parts to a particular package purchased for an evening's meal. The opportunity to track consumption of food and medicines and replace as necessary is already in operation. In Mexico, tests are under way to implant RFID chips in infants to combat the abduction of newborns and small children. Proponents claim RFID can drive operational improvements through better inventory management, manufacturing efficiency, elimination of shrinkage, reduced distribution cycles and cost, and better customer service. The U.S. meat industry suggests that the mad cow disease scare cost the industry $8 billion, a situation that can be quickly diagnosed and minimized in the future through the application of RFID.

Opponents, or more correctly those firms and people trying to understand the full implications, are moving slowly as they cope with the problems, including the physics of RFID, how the information generated will be managed and integrated with legacy data systems, and determining what are and who pays for the costs. Among the already documented problems are coping with heavy metal surroundings and water, and dealing with the pushback regarding security and invasion of privacy. When tags were introduced in a California school, to track students (a tactic already being applied in Japan), a few parents were able to quickly apply pressure and get the school administrators to remove the tags.

But how long can a business remain on the sidelines? With organizations such as Wal-Mart and the U.S. Department of Defense in the forefront, putting their collective endorsement and pressure on finding the benefits of RFID, requiring their key suppliers to be compliant by 2005, many businesses seem to be stuck in the process of evaluating and testing RFID, while a few are moving forward. As these actions play out, the list of promises and problems continues to grow, as does the need to better understand what this is all about.

This book will help the reader comprehend the basics of RFID, the fundamental technology and components, the potential applications and business issues, and the marketplace forces at work in front of and behind the scenes of action. It will explain the links with supply chain management and the need to aid visibility so costs can be reduced and time frames shortened. An outline of the costs that could be involved is presented, along with the potential benefits. Mostly, the book will demystify the issues, as we present a clear roadmap for implementation and adoption by manufacturers, distributors, retailers, and suppliers — to the U.S. Department of Defense and Wal-Mart and virtually any other key member of a supply chain network. Case studies and interviews are included to provide specific illustrations of both early adopter success as well as RFID failures.

While the reader will gain a solid understanding of the technology issues of RFID, emphasis will be placed on overcoming the many problems in harnessing the capabilities that will drive the promises — bottom-line improvement and top-line growth — benefits that will derive from using RFID as one part of achieving total network visibility. The one strategy that must then be accepted is to begin the learning process now and determine, on a test basis, where the technology can introduce business and personal improvements and how a reasonable return on investment can be made on the applications.

CONTENTS

This book begins with a brief introduction to the basics of the RFID technology and the components of an RFID system. Technical and compliance issues are covered so the reader has grounding in what is behind building an operating system and to aid in the development of long-term strategies for RFID systems management. The differences between RFID and other automatic identification technologies are covered, as are the issues surrounding acceptance and implementation. Thus far, too much emphasis has been placed on mandatory compliance. The real issue is how businesses should use compliance in order to rationally and effectively test, deploy, and integrate RFID, finding logical applications and business benefits in the process. We progress with a description of the market forces driving and restricting adoption, with particular coverage of the impact by two of the largest buying organizations in the world — Wal-Mart and the U.S. Department of Defense. Details of what these two drivers intend to accomplish and the motives behind their actions are described.

Drawing on the foundation established, we explain how RFID is being deployed by a few pathfinders and compliant suppliers to improve internal processing and supply chain management. Potential uses and nonuses will be outlined, as arguments from the advocates and cynics are considered before endorsing a go-forward position. Once a strong case for action is developed, using RFID as a part of total supply chain visibility, strategy and implications for a business are considered, as we merge the promises — overt and less obvious — that are fueling the advocacy and the pitfalls that are holding back wider scale endorsement into a viable business plan. Positives and negatives will continue to be considered as we explain how a business can deploy applications using the technology with the expectation of gaining a reasonable return on the effort.

Subsequent chapters cover the impact of RFID for security applications and how it will provide safer conditions within supply chain processing. Special attention is given to two business areas, first within the defense sector and then the retail sector and the many suppliers to those industries. Since we believe the technology will become pervasive, we also cover many other industries, from health care to service organizations, that will reap eventual benefits.

Finally, we will show how to build a business case for RFID adoption, with a roadmap for execution. Instructions for constructing a productive RFID pilot, which can document the costs, explain the connection with supply chain visibility, and verify or deny the actual benefits, are provided. The concluding chapter summarizes the main themes of the book and the authors' conclusions. Using the future roadmap, a summary case illustrates the potential enhanced set of circumstances. Overall, our goal is to arm you with the knowledge and understanding necessary to draw meaningful conclusions and to develop viable strategies and action plans for the implications RFID will present in your area of business.

ACKNOWLEDGMENTS

Those individuals who were most helpful in contributing to this text are cited as case studies and interview notes are presented. Special recognition must be given to Ben Cagle, Chuck Davis, Charles Fine, Drew Gant, Steven Goble, Jim Grant, Jason Hughes, John Lamelas, Larry Lapide, Ken Mason, Joe McKinney, Daniel Munyan, Douglas Neal, Joel Polakoff, Richard Poulson, Mark Roberti, Larry Scheuble, Sandy Scott, Yossi Sheffi, Steve Simco, Jim Thompson, and Ian Walker.

Particular thanks should go to all of our clients, from whom we have learned so much.

ABOUT THE AUTHORS

Chuck Poirier is a recognized authority on process improvement, supply chain management, e-business techniques, and the collaborative use of technology around the world. He has written 12 business books, 6 of which are related to improving supply chain processing. His work has been translated into nine languages. In addition to his work as a partner in the Computer Sciences Corporation Supply Chain Practice, he is a frequent presenter at national and international conferences and industry meetings. With more than 40 years of business experience, including senior-level positions, and the extensive research conducted for the writing of his many books, white papers, and position documents, Mr. Poirier is comfortable before any audience seeking help with value chain networks. He has assisted many firms in a variety of industries to establish the framework for their supply chains and to find the hidden values across the collaborative networking that can be established. His advanced techniques have become a hallmark of firms seeking the most benefits from cross-organizational collaboration.

Duncan McCollum is a Principal in Computer Sciences Corporation Global AIT Solutions Group. His responsibilities are focused on RFID project delivery, including proof-of-concept demonstrations, RFID education, business case development, RFID strategy, and systems integration design. He has been involved in a variety of RFID work since 2001 and has experience with low, high, and ultrahigh frequency passive RFID as well as active RFID systems. He frequently speaks in the United States and Europe and writes on issues involving the selection, evaluation, and implementation of RFID technology to a wide variety of audiences and trade groups. His projects have covered Wal-Mart and U.S. Department of Defense compliance, high-value asset tracking, RFID security systems, and the use of RFID for cargo container tracking. Mr. McCollum holds a master's of business administration from Southern Methodist University Cox School of Business and a bachelor's degree from the University of Mississippi. He has served on the Board of Advisors of the Department of Electrical Engineering at Southern Methodist University and is on the Advisory Board of Ripcord Technologies. The industries in which he has specific experience include manufacturing, retail, government, and consumer products.

Free value added materials available from
the Download Resource Center at www.jrosspub.com

At J. Ross Publishing we are committed to providing today's professional with practical, hands-on tools that enhance the learning experience and give readers an opportunity to apply what they have learned. That is why we offer free ancillary materials available for download on this book and all participating Web Added Value™ publications. These online resources may include interactive versions of material that appears in the book or supplemental templates, worksheets, models, plans, case studies, proposals, spreadsheets and assessment tools, among other things. Whenever you see the WAV™ symbol in any of our publications, it means bonus materials accompany the book and are available from the Web Added Value Download Resource Center at www.jrosspub.com.

Downloads available for *RFID Strategic Implementation and ROI: A Practical Roadmap to Success* consist of slides that explain RFID fundamentals and implementation strategy and an RFID roadmap poster.

FUNDAMENTALS OF RFID TECHNOLOGY AND APPLICATIONS

When new technologies are discovered or introduced, there are always two camps, with differing opinions on the values to be gained from implementation. From the time of the Luddites, there have been technology advocates and cynics — supporters and opponents. A clear example of such a condition is provided by the current near-sensational hype and fierce controversy surrounding not only the discovery of radio frequency identification (RFID), which has been around since the middle 1940s, but its recent introduction as a means of providing benefits for a variety of business, commercial, and societal applications. Supply chains, in particular, have become a target area of application, especially as a tool to aid the search for full visibility across an extended enterprise, and they sit squarely in the middle of the controversy.

A strong conflict is already brewing in the supply chain arena, between the proponents, who expect RFID tags to become a replacement for (or at least a complement to) bar codes, and the opponents, who believe the investment does not provide a significant benefit or positive return on investment. In a proactive example, Boeing and Airbus are moving forward as those firms have created one RFID strategy for airplane manufacturing, as a complement to meeting U.S. Department of Defense mandates. The world's largest aircraft, the Airbus 380, moreover, will be equipped with 10,000 RFID tags. The tags will be attached to removable parts of the airplane, to aid the control of maintenance programs. Delta plans to spend $25 million to use RFID to track 2 million pieces of baggage per year and reduce its $60 million cost to retrieve and deliver lost luggage. For the opponents, however, RFID is nothing more than a temporary distraction to be resisted. For this camp, there is sufficient technology already available to get the job done.

DISCUSSION PERSISTS AT BOTH ENDS OF THE DEBATE

The considerations have established a polar set of conditions. At the far end of the spectrum of debate are strong advocates, who see a burgeoning series of nonbusiness applications for RFID, including placing tags in the ears of animals and the heels of babies for tracking throughout a lifetime, milk cartons that signal a need for replacement, and prescription pill boxes that track usage. An equal number of cynics occupy the opposite outer region, including those who are concerned with the tags remaining functional after products have been consumed. For these parties, RFID can be used for further surveillance and intrusions into privacy, and they stand strongly opposed to implementation. They are joined by those claiming the costs will never be recovered by the manufacturers and insufficient technology exists today for all applications.

And so the battle rages, as both sides debate the future of the technology and its potential implementation. Anticipating that the scenario will play out positively has caused the proponents to move quickly forward and mandate application. Obliging suppliers have also tried to move in compliance with these powerful mandates. Anticipating less favorable results has led some of the opposition to push back on compliance demands and try to stall the movement, at least until participants can see what the real costs and benefits might be. In between, there is a plethora of people and businesses that simply do not understand what is happening enough to make any kind of rational movement. Frozen in place describes the bulk of the businesses and people we have surveyed.

In this book, we will present the pertinent facts and application data, so a judicious decision can be made regarding RFID, depending on the circumstances of the market in which a firm does business, the pertinent supply chain factors in the market environment, and the real potential to recover the costs of compliance and RFID action. Throughout the discourse, attention will be given to the promises and problems associated with the new technology and what can be expected as it moves inexorably toward what we see as full-scale adoption within a decade.

The hypothesis that will be in the center of our consideration is that RFID will first become an accepted aid to visibility across business supply chains, and thus become the real driver behind execution — not short-term benefits to retailers and the military. Later, after further research and development and lowering of costs, RFID will be used as a central feature of wireless technology in a state of total network connectivity. In this level of progress, there will be more "things" online than people, and RFID identification will be a crucial element in the resultant network communication system. We will begin with a review of how this technology sprang on the business screen and why it has become such a hot topic. We will also set the stage for where it will progress in a variety of environments, by pointing to the positives and negatives, the promises and problems now and for the future.

HISTORY OF RFID SYSTEMS

According to many researchers, the earliest application of RFID dates to the years near the end of World War II, when the United Kingdom applied such devices to distinguish English airplanes returning from battle from enemy aircraft — a friend or foe situation. The use of radar at the time was limited to providing a signal to indicate an approaching airplane, not the country of origin. In a seminal paper on the subject entitled "Communication by Means of Reflected Power," Harry Stockman predicted that "considerable research and development work has to be done before the remaining basic problems in reflected power communication are solved, and before the field of useful applications is explored" (Stockman 1948).

His was quite a prophecy, as useful applications have taken decades to reach fruition. RFID may be the oldest "new" technology to date. It took 30 years for the technology to become a practical reality, with early applications in livestock tagging and tracing, toll road passes, and security access cards. Before its discovery as an aid to inventory tracking, bar coding appeared and became an accepted business standard for product identification, as did optical character reading and biometric imaging, all progressing the concept of identifying animate or inanimate objects through a scanning device. It took another score of years to bring RFID into focus for business applications, with emphasis on smart labels, memory cards, and inventory management.

An unexpected assist occurred in 1974, when manufacturers and distributors from 12 European countries decided to form an ad hoc council to investigate the possibility of developing a standard numbering system similar to what was in effect through the Universal Product Code (UPC) in the United States. As a result of this preliminary work, the European Article Numbering collaboration was established in 1977 as EAN International, with the headquarters for this nonprofit entity placed in Brussels.

A particularly important move occurred in 1999, when RFID advocates stepped forward and declared that a global network could be created in which tiny microchips attached to antennas and low-cost tags would gather data in an errorless environment and transfer the information contained seamlessly across extended supply chains. The Uniform Code Council (UCC), together with Procter & Gamble and Gillette, provided seed funding for the Auto-ID Center, a nonprofit research organization headquartered at the Massachusetts Institute of Technology in Cambridge, Massachusetts. This entity, which now includes the University of Cambridge in England and the University of Adelaide in Australia, was created to study, promote, and exploit RFID in supply chain applications.

The goal was to develop a very low-cost RFID tag that could be attached to any item and the network to locate, manage, and exchange information about these items (tags), thus creating the building blocks for what was eventually called an "Internet of Things." Over the next two years, the Auto-ID Center grew to include major consumer product goods companies, retailers, government organizations, as well as hardware, software, and consulting providers.

On October 1, 2001, the Auto-ID Center and sponsors introduced the first large-scale field test and application of the new technology at a Sam's Club retail store in Tulsa, Oklahoma. Results of that initial pilot were significant enough to instill action by a prime mover — the largest retailer in the world, Wal-Mart. This action was quickly followed by the U.S. Department of Defense announcing that it would also march down the RFID road.

In October 2003, EAN International and the UCC assumed the administrative functions of the Auto-ID Center, to support the development and deployment of the Electronic Product Code (EPC) network. At the heart of this network was to be the 96-bit EPC, using a string of numbers to identify an item's manufacturer and product category. An organization known as EPCglobal was quickly established to fulfill those aims. EPCglobal's stated goal is to "establish and support the EPC network as the global standard for immediate, automatic, and accurate identification of any item in the supply chain of any company, in any industry, anywhere in the world. Our objective is to drive global adoption of the EPCglobal network" (EPCglobal 2004).

ANTICIPATION LEADS TO A DEBATED CALL FOR ACTION

With the promotion of the potential of the technology by two of the largest procurement groups in the world — Wal-Mart and the U.S. Department of Defense — for reasons to be discussed in separate chapters, mandates to use RFID to track pallets and cartons in those supply chains have introduced a flurry of activity, both positive and negative. It is important to note that similar mandates have been announced by European retailers, such as Tesco in the United Kingdom, Carrefour in France, and Metro AG in Germany, and other U.S.-based firms have entered the mandate business as well, including Albertsons grocery stores, Best Buy, and Target Stores. Without question, these mandates are driving the technology forward, as those who wish to profit from the application are multiplying and providing the tools of execution — chips, tags, readers, antennas, software, middleware, and so forth. An equal and opposite force is at work as well. According to Kara Romanow, of AMR Research, "Many of Wal-Mart's suppliers are convinced that there is no ROI, and even worse, consider their technology investments to be a throwaway" (Gartner 2004).

When Gillette, the Massachusetts-based personal care products company, began exploration of the potential to use the technology to dramatically reduce shrinkage of its valuable pallet loads of replacement razor blades, the effort picked up momentum, and further pilot tests began to appear. When retailers found that RFID could lead to a lesser need for personnel as well as improved stocking (by reducing out-of-stocks at the shelf level), the accelerator was hit again. The U.S. Food and Drug Administration entered the picture with a strong recommendation to use RFID to reduce the amount of drug counterfeiting — 7 percent in the United States, 20 percent in Europe, and 40 percent in Africa.

The U.S. Department of Homeland Security immediately began an investigation of possible RFID technology, in an attempt to authenticate the contents of incoming cargo containers, only 2 percent of which are thoroughly checked. When the military realized the technology could lead to having the right material in the hands of needy war fighters, and also make sure it was not lost but transferred to other theaters of action when the conflict was over, the die was permanently cast and usage was required, first by 2004 and then by 2005, with some of the costs to be covered by the U.S. Department of Defense.

But the controversy also increased. Placing tags that cost 20 to 35 cents on a pallet seemed like an easy way to get started and reduce costs while tracking inventory movement, especially if the tag cost and tag placement expenses are borne solely by the supplier and not the retailer or the military. When the suggestion was made to add such tags to a carton of consumer goods or an individual item, the idea was rejected outright, as the cost would not be recoverable. Recouping the cost per item might be feasible for high-cost items, but cynics questioned the ability to recover costs on inexpensive items. How can you recover the extra cost of a 25-cent label on a tube of toothpaste? Or a container of shoe polish? And so the conflict continues into the future, as further applications are tested and advocates and cynics square off in a match to decide on acceptance or rejection.

RFID DEFINED

Other questions and concerns quickly appeared, requiring resolution. Around what technology and what components does the controversy rage? What is this thing called RFID and where is it headed? These questions need to be answered if we are to progress with meaningful solutions. For the purposes of this book, we will use RFID as a generic term for technologies that use radio waves to automatically identify individual items or artifacts — using what has been termed a form of digital watermark or individual signature. The term EPC refers specifically to passive RFID technology and standards supported by EPCglobal, with particular emphasis on supply-chain-based applications.

To assist in understanding what is behind using this unique digital signature, we turn to Figure 1.1. The diagram and descriptive text elaborate on the vision established for RFID technology. With a chip and antenna (an RFID tag) attached to a pallet, an electronic product code can be sent to a reader for transfer to a savant or other interpretive system. The information can then be used for a variety of purposes or transferred to an online network system and on to other trading partners. In theory, the contents and location of the pallet can be tracked wherever it goes.

For a more detailed view, we turn to Figure 1.2. At its core, RFID becomes a tagging system used to provide electronic identity to any object — a wireless means of gathering and analyzing information about an artifact. From another view, it is meant to serve as a secure means to connect servers that contain information related to items identified by EPC numbers. Data on the object

RFID Tag — Small microchip attached to an antenna, usually embedded as part of an adhesive label that can have bar code and human-readable information printed on it. Tag can be read-only or read-write and carries a unique identification code (EPC).

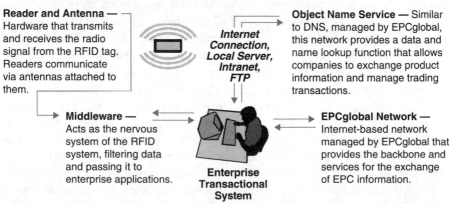

Reader and Antenna — Hardware that transmits and receives the radio signal from the RFID tag. Readers communicate via antennas attached to them.

Internet Connection, Local Server, Intranet, FTP

Object Name Service — Similar to DNS, managed by EPCglobal, this network provides a data and name lookup function that allows companies to exchange product information and manage trading transactions.

Middleware — Acts as the nervous system of the RFID system, filtering data and passing it to enterprise applications.

Enterprise Transactional System

EPCglobal Network — Internet-based network managed by EPCglobal that provides the backbone and services for the exchange of EPC information.

Figure 1.1. How the Technology Works (EPCglobal, Inc. Version)

(serial numbers, object information, etc.) are stored in chips embedded in or attached to the object or placed on its container. Using an RFID reader, the identity of the object can be interpreted in a wireless environment. From a technical viewpoint, RFID becomes a label with an embedded unique EPC, with the following characteristics:

- Standard nomenclature for identifying items via a unique identification broadcast over an appropriate radio frequency.
- EPC and/or other information stored on a microchip that is attached to an antenna; the chip and the antenna together are called a transponder or more commonly an RFID tag.
- Readable tags that may be passive, with power supplied from the reader, or active, with a power source within the tag. Semi-passive tags use an integral battery to run the chip's circuitry but draw power from the reader to communicate.
- Tags that can be read while in motion without a line of sight.
- Tags that are small enough to be applied as a label on most items.

From another technical aspect, a transponder is a specific point on the radio spectrum tuned to a receiver via its special antennas. A series of transponders and receivers constitute a working system, normally operating at the same frequency to provide data exchange features. Typical components of such a system include:

- RFID tags, ranging in size from a person's palm to a pinhead, that contain a small radio frequency chip coupled to a microprocessor (i.e., devices made from an electronic circuit, carrying identification and other data about the item, which can be broadcast upon receiving a request from a reader that operates on the same frequency and protocol used with the tag). The radio frequency is used to transfer the data. The tag contains portable memory (normally 8k to 256k) in a read-only or read/write mode and is usually attached to specific items. In some situations, the transceiver and tag operate as a single unit.
- Antennas to transmit and receive the electromagnetic waves through wireless transfer as data.
- Readers or radio frequency transceivers used to send information to the tag and receive back data from the tag. The reader communicates with the tag via the antenna, receives commands from application software, transforms radio waves into digital information, and provides a power supply to passive tags.
- Application software to perform a specific function, such as keeping track of products and inventory (in transit or storage), placing re-orders, or issuing instructions to restock. The software could also

4. Arriving products at a DC are automatically detected by readers at the unloading docks. Product is received, recorded, and allocated against orders. **Cross-docking operations** are streamlined by matching product receipts with outbound shipments. Unallocated product can be dynamically slotted, increasing warehouse efficiency.

3. Shipping can be improved by automatically verifying pallet-level RFID reads to shipping manifests.

2. RFID tags facilitate manufacturing by enabling seamless tracking and retrieval of RM. Companies that integrate their RFID technology with the production scheduling systems can perform real-time checks for materials in RM. WIP to help better schedule production. Manufacturers can tag the finished product in final assembly or later in distribution.

1. Raw materials (RM) with an RFID tag are automatically received, greatly reducing the time and inaccuracies associated with manual inspections, three-way matching, and data entry. Products are directly loaded into inventory systems, allowing for the release of production orders and an uninterrupted flow (for JIT environments). RFID can also facilitate dynamic stocking.

5. Sensors at various points in the supply chain distribution network can provide information and alerts about temperature, humidity, shock, and other preset alerts.

6. RFID increases the effectiveness of a **warehouse management system** by facilitating dynamic slotting, inventory accuracy, and pick routes. By tracking every movement of a product, the WMS is in sync with the other DC applications.

7. RFID benefits the customer by **facilitating** the following activities:
- Product loaded on the outbound vehicle can be validated based on tag data
- RFID technology can integrate with the creation of key shipping documents (e.g., BOL, ASN, CSO)

8. RFID increases the transparency of goods in transit by relaying real-time shipment **tracking** information. Most of this functionality is provided by carriers. The lot tracking points are made better from a recall management point.

9. Retail product tracking is improved through the use of RFID. Tagged product can be tracked from backroom to retail space to checkout. Empty shelves and misplaced product can be communicated and located throughout the network.

10. One of the most important applications of RFID is in the **replenishment process.** Inventory levels can be balanced against in-transit orders, resulting in a clear picture of the replenishment profile.

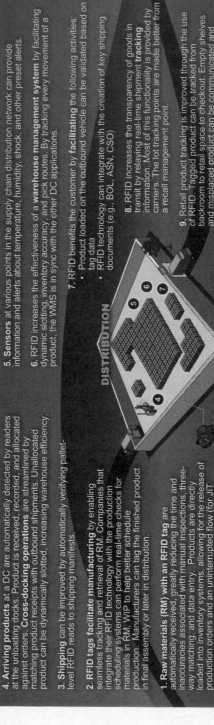

DISTRIBUTION

RFID Middleware

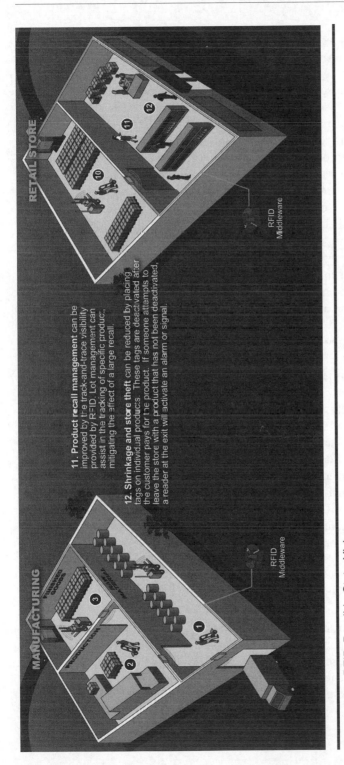

11. Product recall management can be improved by the track-and-trace visibility provided by RFID. Lot management can assist in the tracking of specific product, mitigating the effect of a large recall.

12. Shrinkage and store theft can be reduced by placing tags on individual products. These tags are deactivated after the customer pays for the product. If someone attempts to leave the store with a product that has not been deactivated, a reader at the exit will activate an alarm or signal.

Figure 1.2. RFID Possible-State Vision

send data to specific readers to write other data on tags, like the sale of the item, an important movement event, or the presence of an empty pallet.

- Middleware to sort through the data and pass on whatever is relevant. Middleware is essentially the adhesive that binds hardware components from lower layers with higher application layers. It performs such functions as making read/write commands more reliable and transferring and routing data through readers to the correct location. Middleware can also act as the watchdog of the system by providing alerts and routing based on real-time location and quantity information. For example, if a retailer wants to maintain a certain level of product (either at the item level on the shelf or at the case or pallet level in a warehouse), rules can be built into the middleware to send a restocking alert when levels fall below a prescribed limit.

- Host computer that reads/writes the data from or to the tags through the reader, stores and evaluates data obtained, and links the transceivers to an application, such as an enterprise resource planning system.

RFID tags have gone through numerous developmental phases, and the current "Generation 2 EPC tag" contains a header with 8 bits to determine the structure of the subsequent series of numbers, a domain manager with 28 bits to identify the company or entity responsible for maintaining the subsequent numbers, an object class with 24 bits to identify an object class representing a group of products, and a serial number with 36 bits containing a unique object identification. As tags increase in sophistication, they can start to resemble Bluetooth or wireless fidelity (Wi-Fi) chips. In such an instance, they could be powered and specialized for customized applications. One element driving adoption is the fact that these tags can function without batteries and have a long life and require little maintenance. Additional information on the applicable standards, frequencies, and hierarchy of components is provided in the Appendix, along with other pertinent technical data.

HOW DOES AN RFID SYSTEM WORK?

A typical RFID system is illustrated in summary fashion in Figure 1.3, where we see the basic components arrayed once again. The process begins with an active or passive chip used to instigate the system. The antenna enables the chip to transmit the identification information to the reader, which converts the radio waves returned from the tag into a form that can be passed on to computers

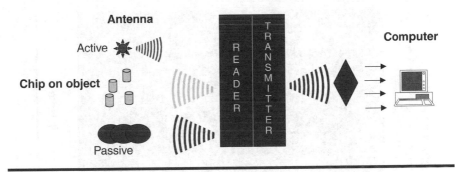

Figure 1.3. RFID: How It Works

that can make use of the data. Virtually all systems operate with these fundamental ingredients. As supply chains incorporate the technology, the process
diagram moves closer to what was displayed in Figure 1.2.

In a hypothetical 16-step process, or conditions used for industrial and
commercial purpose, the figure follows the preliminary attachment of an RFID
tag to a product such as cartons of paper at a paper mill. With these tags, the
identity and count of the product can be tracked, even when packaged or
wrapped. As pallets of the paper cartons begin to leave the manufacturer, a
reader powers the tags. The tags can now broadcast their unique EPCs. In the
illustration, the reader is wired into a computer system, where the EPC is
collected and processed by a savant (essentially software that acts as the nervous
system of an EPC network). Using the Internet, the tracking continues, possibly
around the globe, but certainly across the extended supply chain.

When the paper arrives at a distribution center, the tags are read again
without the necessity to open the cartons. The paper continues on to its next
stop. At the retail outlet, where the shipment has been tracked as described,
information is brought up to date. Inventory can now be tracked accurately in
real time. With retail shelves also equipped with readers, the system understands
when paper is added to stock or display or taken away, tracking consumption
and replenishment. With this system, the consumer has an easier time, by
allowing a reader to record the purchase and take payment through a swipe of
a credit card. Inside the consumer's house, a computer updates additions and
deletions as well, adding a replacement to the shopping list when appropriate.

The major concern, of course, revolves around the cost of the system necessary to accomplish the illustrated tracking. Figure 1.4 describes the hierarchy
of such costs, from the Class 0/Class 1 passive tags to Class 5 tags with readers.
The least expensive passive RFID tags range from low 10-cent to mid-30-cent

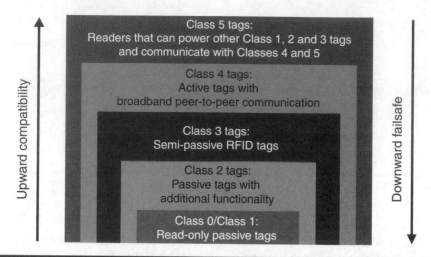

Figure 1.4.   RFID Tags Range in Capability and Price

based on purchase volume. Advocates see the day when 5- to 10-cent tags are in broad use. Procter & Gamble expects that a 10-cent tag will justify pallet- and case-level tagging and tracking.

When the cost of readers and other parts of an RFID system is included, the price goes higher, however, typically in the range of $50,000 to $250,000 per installed site. But the potential usage could have great impact on costs in the future as larger scales are achieved. It was estimated that the 14 original commercial users that were the founding members of the Auto-ID Center would consume 412 billion RFID tags each year, if they chose to tag all the objects they produce. In addition, the U.S. Postal Service would require over 200 billion tags for the objects it handles in a year.

PROMISES OF RFID

From those who endorse such a system, there are many benefits to be derived from the use of RFID, which will be described throughout this text. They begin with the ability to communicate object-specific information on products and artifacts as they move anywhere in the world. What is envisioned by the pro- ponents is a worldwide network of data that tracks real-time movement, par- ticularly knowledge useful for authentication and authorization (i.e., to elimi- nate counterfeiting and theft). Advocates also cite a series of more obvious technical benefits, including:

- Line of sight is not needed, as is required in the use of bar coding, making tracking easier.
- A reader can scan multiple tags, as many as 1,000 at a time with current technology.
- It is not necessary to manually orient the goods being scanned toward the reader for correct operation.
- RFID radio energy can usually penetrate a retail item's packaging and ascertain what is inside, although water and metal present current problems.
- Tags embedded in the package cannot be scuffed, scraped, rubbed off, or damaged.
- Tags can contain several times the amount of information as bar codes.
- Capability exists to write and store further information on the tags.
- Dramatic improvement in information flexibility occurs (i.e., changing information on the tags) as goods move across the supply chain network.

In addition to the technical features of an RFID system, advocates look to a future state where members of an extended enterprise can go to a central network system and have visibility into what has taken place across an end-to-end supply, manufacturing, delivery, and replenishment system. The ability to capture data in a hands-free manner and to accumulate information from a variety of products in one place certainly holds value for inventory management systems, as the inventory can literally talk to the observer. Cycle times could be improved as it takes less time to replenish shipments. Keeping the information secure and traceable offers advantages in today's business environment, especially as it establishes authentication to the shipments. According to Kevin Ashton, the former executive director of the Auto-ID Center, there is a future "where physical objects communicate with one another in real time, where trading partners know exactly where their products are at every point in the supply chain, where information finally triumphs over inventory" (Quinn 2003).

From our viewpoint, acceptance of RFID ushers in a new era in communication and knowledge exchange, as it expands the ability to create visibility into the transfer of assets and moves the wireless world one step further along. These capabilities will be discussed in detail in subsequent chapters. For now, we stand with the advocacy, as we envision so many positive aspects to the use of the RFID technology.

From an economic view, RFID will cut labor costs involved in data collection and back office functions and facilitate warranty return tracking and handling. Working capital should be improved as fewer assets are lost and inventory is more visible and safety stocks shrink. These matters are covered in detail in Chapter 3. As the positives are accumulated, however, we strongly advise that the application not become viewed as a panacea. RFID is at its heart an enabler to better capture and transfer data. The real value is yet to be realized, through its position as a catalyst within a supply chain information system and as part of a wireless business environment.

PROBLEMS WITH RFID

There are also those who are not yet convinced of the ubiquitous or fortuitous future of RFID. Sunder Kekre, professor at Carnegie-Mellon University, summarizes some of the caution being expressed as he states: "RFID will generate vast amounts of data. But how will you utilize that data to predict problems, isolate issues, and improve processes to drive efficiencies and create value? We need better methods for developing business intelligence" (Kekre 2004).

Brian Zrimsek, vice president of research for Gartner, speaking at the Symposium 2004 conference in Sydney, Australia, painted an even bleaker picture. He warned that current RFID deployments merely enhance established business processes, citing the fact that Wal-Mart's RFID dictate to its suppliers did not meet a critical business process test known as "act-on-fact." This term refers to the point in a supply chain process where the firm is able to "execute an order the moment it comes in," rather than in minutes, hours, or days. Zrimsek avows, "I don't think we will see mass RFID until at least 2010. RFID trophy case Wal-Mart is working on a tactical rather than strategic solution. It's basically another labeling system" (Zrimsek 2004).

RFID technology has received more than its share of resistance and pushback, including concerns about the higher costs versus bar coding, the need to engage in reengineering and restructuring, and issues pertaining to privacy and security. The primary argument against the use of RFID begins when opponents point out the near universal use of bar coding as an accepted practice. Why do we need a tag? What benefit do I derive from an investment in RFID? Among the many responses, we point out that RFID provides automatic capture of data at a unique item level in an unattended, high-speed, and hands-free manner. As the technology improves, the read range and read rate capability will continue to increase. Most importantly, it is a means of having the inventory talk to you and withstand harsh or dirty environments.

Concerns have been raised from a technical viewpoint regarding the limitations of RFID systems for global applications because of various frequency ranges, the absence of regulation and standards, and the interference from residual radio frequency sources. There is also the need for complementary technologies to keep pace. Processes for embossing and packaging the chips need to become more economical. Improvements in the cost of readers, possibly falling below $25, are expected. These and other technical factors will no doubt be resolved in the next few years. A greater concern is for the interference with reading tags in difficult media, like metal and water (foil packaging and liquid detergents), which could delay movement in some important areas.

From a less technical aspect, there will be nagging concerns surrounding what will happen with large-scale adoption and the sudden presence of large volumes of new data. How will this data be accumulated and shared? Who will retain ownership of the information? How can the dangerous elements be kept secure? Who will be able to gain access? Any new system would need to be integrated with legacy systems that contain an equal amount of information. If Wal-Mart were to tag all of its retail products in the United States, for example, its information technology system could be inundated with an additional 7.7 terabytes of data each day (Violino 2003).

From a general viewpoint, other challenges include:

- Determining the correct application for such a wide variety of possible uses
- Dealing with the concern for privacy, which becomes more transparent with wide RFID usage
- Resolving the technology and standards issues on a global basis
- Integrating the technology in a logical and economical manner with current business practices
- Getting beyond the pilots into solid, actionable case studies that document the costs and benefits

APPLICATIONS ARE PAVING THE WAY TO ACCEPTANCE

In spite of the opposition, some current applications are beginning to pave the roadway forward. By embedding tags in cartons or affixing them to pallets, a user can identify what is in the box or on the pallet and track it as it moves. Information about the contents can be read at multiple locations, with time notations when the box or pallet passes a particular location. With this data, companies can do a better job of planning. Not only is this good news for those in supply chains, but it can be a boon for border security and post-9/11 concerns about international shipments. Tracking the specific animal that sparked the mad cow scare was aided by RFID technology. The ability to separate real from counterfeit items and other applications have brought the technology onto the front pages.

Low-frequency RFID tags have been in use for some time for animal identification, tracking movement of beer kegs and rolls of paper, and automobile antitheft systems. Pets have been embedded with small chips so they can be identified when lost and returned to their owners. Michelin, the tire company, has been using RFID transponders in its tires so carmakers and dealers can track inventory or specific tires mounted on specific cars. One idea is to send a signal when a tire needs to be rotated or replaced. RFID smart cards are widely used in Hong Kong, the Netherlands, and Malaysia for mass transit fare payment. The major issue is not whether there are applications but how far the applications will go and what the overall business value is.

RFID has been positioned on the one hand as a replacement for UPC (a 25-year-old technology) bar codes. The RFID code is long enough, for example, to enable a unique code for each item versus identification at the lot or SKU level, as is customary with bar codes. But is that necessary? UPC codes are limited to a single code for all instances of a particular product, which has been sufficient for most consumer goods applications. RFID tags may be tracked from location to location, offering another advantage for inventory tracking. Perhaps there is an advantage over the more traditional UPC code, but more work is necessary to resolve this part of the conflict.

As Sherry Aaholm, senior VP at FedEx Corp., told an audience at the *Information Week* Spring 2004 Conference: "It would be monumental for us to replace the bar-code technology, so we'll start off with RFID as a supplemental offering with some suppliers." When asked about loading value-added data on tags in the near future, she added, "It's a closed loop currently for RFID between our distribution partners and us. We expect to deal with whole different levels of privacy and security concerns next year when we make much more information available through radio frequency" (Garvey 2004). We find these comments indicative of the trend toward acceptance of the technology, coupled with business wariness about the issues needing further clarification.

EPCglobal is working on proposed international standards, which if accepted could add further impetus to the RFID movement. The U.S. Food and Drug Administration also has RFID under the microscope, as it moves toward ruling on whether hospitals can use RFID systems to identify patients, allow relevant staff to access and peruse medical records, and authenticate the pedigree of prescription medicine.

Helping the proponent camp in the debate over implementation is the news that the cost of the chip continues to drop, now pegged at about five cents. But the chip needs to be attached to something, and companies like Avery-Dennison will be happy to oblige with a label or appropriate device that can be connected with the product or pallet. Then a reader and antenna and all the other components must be bought and put into place. From a nickel to 25 cents or several dollars per item, the cost-benefit ratio must be developed as the technology is moved from pallets and gets closer to individual items.

From a negative aspect, the use of RFID has created considerable controversy in some quarters and even instigated product boycotts. In perhaps the most notable case of RFID and consumer privacy concerns, Gillette, the personal care products company, was the focus of negative publicity for a pilot test conducted at a Wal-Mart store in Brockton, Massachusetts. Gillette Mach3 razor blades are among the most frequently shoplifted items from retail shelves. In an effort to experiment with the capability of RFID to track items at the shelf level, Gillette and Wal-Mart proposed a test to tag individual units of Mach3 razor kits. The proposed benefits of the test were to alert store management when restocking needed to occur and if an unusually high quantity of items was removed from the shelf (an indication of a shoplifting incident).

Before going live, however, Wal-Mart decided to stop the test in order to focus resources on current work within its distribution centers and activities with suppliers related to its recently announced RFID mandates. Consumers Against Supermarket Privacy Invasion and Numbering (CASPIAN) picked up the story and launched a website (www.boycottgillette.com) to draw attention to the potential of RFID abuses by retailers and manufacturers. The group urged consumers to boycott all Gillette products and contact Gillette management, as well as legislators, with their concerns.

CASPIAN's efforts have raised awareness of RFID and consumer privacy concerns enough that several states are currently looking at what, if any, legislation is required in this area — to protect consumers. Additionally, EPCglobal has established a working group on privacy issues and recommended that all packaging that is tagged with an EPCglobal RFID tag also include a consumer awareness notice. For any company considering using RFID at any consumer unit purchase level, thorough consideration should be given to developing an RFID and consumer privacy strategy, much as a privacy policy is incorporated as part of a company's website presence. It should be noted that Gillette did go forward with a test, including a miniature camera to take a picture of the person removing the Mach3 units from the shelf, with Metro in Germany.

The primary privacy concerns include:

■ The buyer of an item might not be aware of the presence of the tag or be able to remove it.

- The tag can be read at a distance without the knowledge or approval of the owner.
- When the item is bought with a credit card, it would be possible to attach the ID of the item to the buyer.
- Tags can establish globally unique serial numbers for all products, even though this disturbs privacy advocates and is deemed unnecessary for most applications.
- RFID tags remain affixed to products and continue to be functional after products have been purchased and taken home, where they can be used for surveillance.

SUMMARY

Make no mistake — RFID is an emerging technology which we predict will be disruptive as it is rapidly introduced and accepted by various sectors of the business and commercial world. The necessity is to sort through the hype and excitement, to find the real business and societal benefits, which will positively position RFID as a useful tool in an identification and visibility network system. There are and will continue to be two camps, both advocates and cynics. Currently, the naysayers seem to occupy the high ground, with more troops and a host of complications and problems to be resolved before they change positions. Most companies are on the sidelines watching what is happening before making commitments to participate. The risks still outweigh the understood advantages for most observers. The cost of the chip is being heralded as a watermark for inducing acceptance, but it is just one element in the system needed to apply RFID technology in a meaningful way. In subsequent chapters, we will consider why this technology is inevitable and how it will find its way ubiquitously into supply chain applications across a myriad of businesses and industries.

2

MARKET FORCES DRIVING AND OBSTRUCTING ADOPTION OF RFID

With the introduction of any new technology, there are a series of qualifying questions seeking answers. Such a series confronts the acceptance of RFID technology. Why is RFID such a hot topic, if there are equal amounts of support and resistance? What is driving its adoption by a majority of the global 2000 businesses and the U.S. government? Will the forces of resistance stop the movement? Within what time frame will proof or disproof no longer be an issue? These and other questions demand attention and response before there will be pervasive application of RFID technology. Amid all the pros and cons, there must be a line toward reality and a defined path, no matter how twisting, that will lead to final resolution and successful application.

According to Mark Roberti, editor of the *RFID Journal,* there is no killer application behind acceptance of the technology. Rather, RFID is an enabling tool, which will enhance many applications. New savings from several of these applications will eventually offset the investment and show the way to reasonable return on effort. When implementation grows, for example, out-of-stocks may become the exception, helping retailers to save much of the 4 percent annually relegated to this business problem. Bear in mind that a 1 percent increase in sales for a company the size of Wal-Mart is equivalent to almost $3 billion in new annual sales. What is desperately needed by the advocates is a further series of stories documenting successful applications. The malingerers waiting on the sidelines are only going to enter the arena when they see positive benefits for participation in their area.

In this chapter, we will explain the forces at work in front of and behind the scenes — as market drivers for acceptance or rejection of RFID systems. We will describe how there is much more than the mandates from Wal-Mart and the U.S. Department of Defense (DOD) bringing attention to this technology. We will also discuss the inhibitions and resistance to full-scale implementation, considering, for example, the needs for improvement in technology performance and costs, a better definition of the role of middleware, and falling RFID tag prices. Along with presenting the forward forces, we will take a serious look at the problems and obstacles retarding RFID adoption.

RFID IS ALREADY IN PLACE

Before introducing our premises either supporting or disputing the use of RFID technology, it is important to recognize that implementation has already been started and accepted in some sectors of society and the business world. As mentioned earlier, RFID has been around since the end of World War II, and applications have been growing, well beyond the publicized business transactions between manufacturers and retailers and the DOD. There is evidence that the basic RFID technology is being pursued in enough areas that it can be considered an accepted tool, albeit one that is far from reaching full potential. For example, consider the number and names of companies taking an active part in the technology application; more than 50 companies make RFID equipment, including Texas Instruments and Philips Electronics, with more in the developmental stages.

There is a very good chance that every reader of this text has already been in contact with an RFID tag and reader. The technology was used at the Academy Awards ceremony for security purposes. Highway tollbooth passes are now a standard application. Exxon Mobil's speed pass and McDonald's acceptance of that pass for payment for burgers and fries is another. Tags are now used as part of electronic car keys for virtually all cars sold in Europe after 1998, effectively reducing car thefts in that sector by 50 percent. Libraries are installing RFID systems to trigger alarms if someone attempts to steal a book and also to find lost volumes and purge those not being read. In just about every office building, RFID "smart cards" are used to gain access to secure areas. Elementary schools in Japan are using RFID to record the arrival and departure of children and to send e-mail confirmation to parents.

A Canadian municipality is using RFID tags as part of a system to bill citizens by the pound for garbage removal. During the 2004 holiday season, toy company Little Tikes introduced a product called MagiCook Kitchen, featuring a plastic stove with an RFID reader and pretend food with embedded tags. The reader identifies the food items placed on the play stove and sets off prerecorded instructions for the child to follow. Disney is now attaching RFID tags to much of its product sent to major customer Wal-Mart and using the technology to prevent the production of counterfeit Disney products. Ford Motor Company affixes RFID tags to help manage the production of its Windstar minivans in Ontario. "The tags are attached to the radiator assemblies of the minivans and provide information about each minivan's specifications to computers and assembly workers throughout the 25-hour production process. They tell robot painters what color to use and let workers know which options, trim combinations, and special components have been ordered on a specific vehicle" (Delaney 2002). For those who thought acceptance of the technology would take decades, another look is in order. RFID is all around us.

We are witnessing the early stages of an unstoppable technology introduction, replete with the usual promises and problems. Applications and new stories appear weekly in the media and journals, tracking progress with RFID technology. In spite of the confusion surrounding costs, risk, getting adequate returns, and how far to proceed, there is enough momentum that our advice is to select the application that has the most promise and begin a test to validate the costs and benefits. In the interim, continue to watch closely as we see the market drivers push the effort forward.

We also advise not to be deterred by skepticism. Early adopters may be the subjects of criticism, but they will gain the high business ground as a reward for their efforts. RFID applications across most industries are still in an immature stage, and testing is no doubt required for forward movement. Those firms willing to experiment and pilot now will have the knowledge needed when the movement becomes pervasive. Suppliers will no doubt pay a large part of the cost for tag and label development and to overcome the problems with foils, water, and proper placement, but again with no set practices, learning will go to those willing to be pathfinders. They will have the benefit of being in an enviable position when customers seek to exchange data on how to benefit from RFID applications.

PRIMARY MARKETS AND THEIR FORCES

To position the topic being considered, we define market forces as the external influences that cause an organization or business to adapt or change in order to remain competitive. While there are many market forces driving RFID implementation, we will consider four primary forces, which are in the forefront of the advocacy part of the technology application (with more certain to develop) and the solutions being sought:

- **DOD** — The DOD is searching for aids to asset visibility (where the things needed by the war fighter are), deployment (how to get them to the theater of need), and life cycle management (how to prevent redundant ordering, transportation, and the cost of obsolescence). The DOD does not want another situation like that which followed Operation Desert Storm, when a huge cache of supplies was no longer needed in that theater and seemed to disappear. It wants a mechanism to track the $80 billion of supplies in the DOD system anywhere in the world. Chapter 6 is devoted to an elaboration of the concerns and possible solutions in this area.

- **Pharmaceuticals** — This industry and life sciences in general are seeking to track shipments from manufacturers through distributors to pharmacies and final consumption, to eliminate sale of counterfeit products and to ensure proper medication is delivered. They need a way to find out exactly what has been produced and prepared for use and by which manufacturer. There is also a need to facilitate product recall and traceability. The interests include increased asset security and invisible asset tags. Some want to make sure the right medicines are taken by the right person at the right time in the right dosages — a simple extension of supply chain logic.

- **Retailers** — This group represents another primary driver, but one receiving the most resistance from upstream suppliers. Retailers are looking to drive down supply chain costs, reduce the need for checking and stocking personnel, eliminate out-of-stock conditions, and reduce shrinkage. They also expect to see significant reductions in working capital requirements through recovery of lost assets, lower inventory, and less need for infrastructure. From a sales perspective, retailers want to increase revenues by eliminating stock-outs of hot-selling items. So far, this group has been foisting costs and implementation upstream and onto suppliers. It remains to be seen how much the eventual costs and savings will be shared as the benefits are measured.

- **Security** — The effects of 9/11 were just one more force behind the growing need for greater security and protection from terrorism. When the desired asset security solutions are combined with the need for reductions in shrinkage, combating counterfeiting, and better safety, this area becomes a prime driver behind RFID. Chapter 5 is devoted to developments in this sector.

The balance of the market drivers cover a broad spectrum of industries and companies, as the knowledge that RFID does have potential payback continues to grow. As we pursue implementation in later chapters, many of these other drivers will be considered. The basic importance of market factors is that they have positive and negative influences that force responses by the business to overcome the threats posed and to leverage the opportunities presented. Analysis of the combined market forces for a particular business will reveal the impact on its business model and the most reasonable internal response.

MARKET OPPORTUNITIES

So what are the real market opportunities? What chance is there for an industry to advocate implementation and not bankrupt the member companies? To begin on the positive side, the advocates are painting a promising future, full of potential benefits. Figure 2.1 illustrates the possible market opportunities for a number of industries. The potential savings have been arrayed against the ability to create movement toward the use of RFID. The DOD and aerospace and

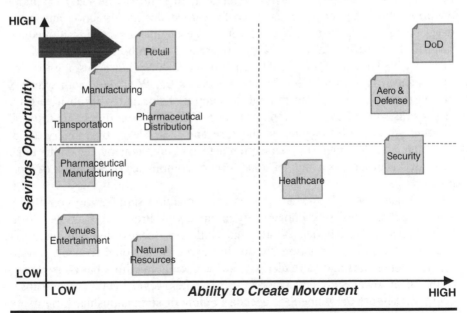

Figure 2.1. RFID Industry Market Opportunity Analysis (Source: Computer Sciences Corporation)

defense are considered the industries with the highest possible return and the most likely to find acceptance. The DOD has so many applications that a special chapter is devoted to that sector. Tracking parts needed by specific airplanes, for example, can be facilitated with the use of RFID tagging systems and represents one application for this business sector. Health care and security are also expected to find a high rate of acceptance, but not the same degree of savings.

Clustered near the lower side of the ability to create movement and with lower savings opportunity are pharmaceutical manufacturing, entertainment, and natural resources. At the upper end of the scale with highest savings opportunity are retail, manufacturing, transportation, and pharmaceutical distribution. In later chapters, we will review all of these groups and explain their incentives and expected resistance to RFID application. The matrix will continue to fill up as more industries move down the inevitable path toward some version of implementation.

FORCEFUL MANDATES ARE DRIVING ACCEPTANCE

For the present, there can be no doubt that, in spite of the need for more documentation, the movement will go forward under the direction and mandates being foisted by a number of very large companies seeking immediate benefits from RFID. In a chronological order, the leading organizations demanding implementation of RFID technology and compliance to some form of implementation are on record by issuing mandates. Wal-Mart, with over six billion cases per year going through its supply chain, and with positive pilot test results, started the ball rolling in June 2003 with a notice to its top 100 suppliers to be RFID enabled at the case and pallet level by January 2005. Subsequently, 36 other suppliers offered to be compliant by the same time. Most of this group has achieved some form of compliance on a portion of their products.

In August 2003, Wal-Mart ordered the remaining suppliers to comply by January 2006. Pilots were immediately initiated with Procter & Gamble, Coca-Cola, Gillette, Kraft Foods, Nestlé, and Unilever. Because the tags were expected to transmit information, the retailer expected it would reduce the need for warehouse staff and store clerks to swipe each item with a bar code reader, resulting in lower staff and labor costs. The item-level mandate was subsequently taken off the immediate agenda in view of serious pushback by many of the suppliers.

The DOD followed in September 2003 with a notice to its top suppliers to be enabled at the case, pallet, and item packaging levels by January 2005. All suppliers were to conduct initial implementation projects by May 2004. Active and passive tags were to be used as supplements to current tags used on containers, with the product value dictating the type of tag to be used. Subsequently, the DOD issued instructions that suppliers should favor passive tags and implement against final policy by January 2005, effective with shipments in October 2005. Greater detail appears in the chapter on this important sector.

A number of other retailers got into the act, beginning with Tesco, the U.K.-based retailer, which issued instruction for certain suppliers to be RFID enabled at the case level by September 2004. Tesco and Gillette have subsequently tested RFID in Cambridge. Gillette believes its sales could jump 15 percent if store shelves were always stocked and thievery stopped (Khermouch and Green 2003, p. 42). A typical retailer, we should note, loses about 4 percent of sales due to being out of stock each year.

Metro AG, the German retailer, wanted its top 100 suppliers enabled at the pallet and transport packaging levels by November 2004. This retailer also established a test market to identify issues with the customer experience in its stores. Target, the Minneapolis-based retailer, wanted its top suppliers enabled at the pallet and case level by spring 2005 and the remaining suppliers on board by spring 2007. Albertsons, the Boise, Idaho–based supermarket retailer, told its top 100 suppliers to be RFID enabled by April 2005.

In addition, the U.S. Food and Drug Administration (FDA) started a task force in 2003 with an antiterrorism focus and an intention to use RFID as an anticounterfeiting measure by 2007 on all packages. Counterfeiting is a growing problem in the life sciences arena. The amount of such activity is estimated to range between 2 and 10% of all goods sold, with a market value between $6.5 and $32.7 billion. The number of open FDA cases relating to counterfeit drugs increased from 6 in 1997 to 22 in 2002. Investigations have netted 44 arrests and 27 convictions, with a number of investigations still pending.

Home Depot also came along and told suppliers they must adopt UCCnet product registry standards by June 30, 2005. "We're going to shut off the manual process and go with an all electronic solution," said Mark Healy, senior director of merchandise operations. For these advocates, a scenario similar to that displayed in Figure 2.2 is on the near horizon. From manufacturing through the delivery process, opportunities will be identified for finding the real advantages and the payback on the necessary investments.

RFID CHALLENGES

Opposed to the advocates are those pointing to existing problems. Andrew White of Gartner Research voices strong opposition, saying, "RFID is the most

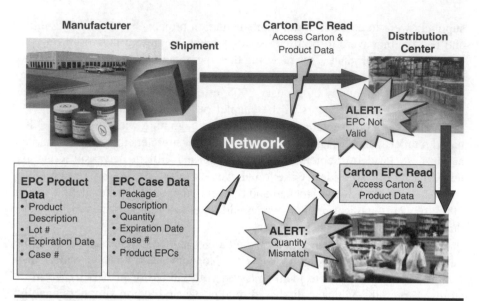

Figure 2.2.   Potential Vision to Secure Supply Chain

over-hyped technology in the supply-chain world." He sees the problems as being "legion," citing such complications as tags being too expensive for wide use, cartons in the interior of pallets being unreadable, and privacy concerns threatening to limit the use of RFID "beyond the retailer's backroom." White states: "Whatever gets deployed in the next year or two will not be an RFID system that every other manufacturer or retailer in the supply chain can use. What little benefit that may accrue will go to Wal-Mart, not go to the supplier" (Foster 2004, p. 39).

Other serious challenges deal with the speed at which many mandates are to be met and the high initial costs that must be incurred without a rational analysis supporting return on investment. With the time deadlines arriving and some suppliers missing the edicts, there seems to be a rush by many suppliers to get compliant without determining the payback on the costs. This situation explains why many of the suppliers in the initial Wal-Mart rollout have adopted a "slap-and-ship" compliance approach — put a label on the pallet and ship it to the demanding customer. Slap and ship minimizes the capital, process, and organizational investment required to meet an RFID mandate.

Slap and ship can also be called "wait and see," as costs for RFID infrastructure (tags, readers, middleware applications) decrease and as organizations gain knowledge on how to effectively manage the information generated by RFID. In a comment similar to that made by White, Navi Radjou of Forrester

Research cautions: "It is all about compliance with large customers such as Wal-Mart and DOD. Wal-Mart should gain better visibility into its inventory, but from a value chain standpoint, there is no benefit to the supplier" (Foster 2004, p. 39).

Having the right application for the right product, if there is one, seems more important to these cynics. They are also concerned with recovering the cost of implementation, but admit there is a strong possibility that tag costs and other equipment will be reduced as usage increases. In between are companies willing to take a calculated risk. Ace Hardware Corporation began testing RFID in 2004, with hopes of deploying the technology at its 15 distribution centers, says Mike Altendorf, VP of IT for the hardware store chain. He notes that "with the current pricing for RFID deployment, we don't see a clear path to a payback, but we know it will come." His is probably the most expected reaction and decision — accept the technology, give RFID a test, and see what actually results.

During what we term the early technology acceptance phase, or what will happen as suppliers do attempt to meet the mandates, we see a learning curve developing, replete with the usual difficulties. One major complication could be that so many suppliers become disenchanted with the technology in their drive to comply that they withhold the necessary development and testing procedures that will eventually show the values that can be added for buyer and supplier. Similarly, retailers unwilling to share the benefits and the information generated by RFID supply chains will retard RFID adoption. As we will point out throughout this text, the value of RFID comes from acting on the information and sharing the values across an extended enterprise. While the recent mandates have been a boon to RFID hardware, software, and system integrators, acting as a catalyst to quickly jump-start RFID adoption, more focus should be placed on the extra values that could derive from trading partner adoption. We are also concerned with the possibility that an undisciplined rush forward will lead to some poor installations, painting a grim picture for other potential advocates.

The time necessary to gain understanding of the solid values is also an inhibitor. Cautious observers predict that as long as five years will be necessary for a unified effort to take hold, requiring cooperation that is currently marginal at best between development companies, hardware suppliers, software vendors, and industry user groups. Again, Radjou advises: "RFID itself is not going to improve the supply chain performance. Companies need to develop new processes that leverage this technology. Retailers and their vendors need to learn new ways to act on the granular location information" (Foster 2004, p. 39).

We add our agreement and the advice that these same players must begin to broaden their perspective to position the technology not as a means of identifying a shortage or locating a missing product, but as a central tool to creating the kind of full network visibility that will bring benefits to all participants in a supply chain. Instant collaboration on identified situations, bad or good, so a solution can be found or a market offering can be introduced, will be one of the real values when this situation occurs.

As mentioned in Chapter 1, one of the significant advantages of RFID is its ability to track an individual, unique item. This capability, and the fact that RFID does not need line of sight to perform a read, has consumer advocacy groups, legislators, and the Federal Trade Commission worried about potential abuses of the technology. The chief concern is that, unknown to the consumer, an individual's purchase behavior and movements can be monitored. For instance, if you bought a suit that had an RFID tag embedded in the shoulder pad, and if the retailer had the appropriate reader/antenna infrastructure in the store, the retailer could not only greet you by name as you enter the store, but could track you as you move throughout the store.

On the one hand, if you were aware that your clothing had this information embedded (a simple ID number that could be associated with your personal and purchasing information from the retailer's point-of-sale system), this might greatly improve and speed up your shopping experience. The sales clerk, for example, could direct you to the items and sizes you typically purchase. On the other hand, as the privacy advocates argue, the potential to abuse this information as well as the potential for malicious third parties to hack into or steal your personal data is too great. The clerk could input information on your purchases and you could be inundated with notices about matching accessories or follow-up advice on the next appropriate purchase to complete your wardrobe.

Other worst-case scenarios could include:

- A disgruntled spouse in a malicious divorce suit standing outside the door to the house scanning all the possessions inside.
- Corporate espionage agents spying on a competitor's new product introduction and sales movement, via wireless reading of distribution centers and retail locations.
- Malicious hacking of RFID tags to destroy or change the information on the tag. In one such scenario, an electronic price-hacker could reduce the price of items before checkout.

What we have is another set of issues that highlight the division RFID has created. Advocates argue that RFID will ultimately benefit the consumer by lowering prices, improving security, and enhancing the shopping experience. Cynics argue that the potential for abuse far outweighs the possible benefits and technical safeguards, and legislation needs to be in place. Somewhere in between there exists a scenario that a firm can adopt to reap benefits without disturbing the privacy enthusiasts.

Both parties are, of course, right. As we gain experience with RFID technology through pilot situations and actual implementations, and consumer education increases, a middle ground will no doubt be reached. A good example of this situation is the approach we use as individuals and organizations regarding e-mail and computer security. We are aware that the potential exists for our systems to be compromised by malicious parties. We also accept the responsibility to select the appropriate level of system security. A similar approach is necessary for RFID. The system manufacturers should ensure that their products and systems are intrinsically safe. We, as consumers, should understand the trade-offs between the benefits and risk.

Other groups call for restraint as the technology and standards are further developed. From our view, the most difficult obstacle is the limited number of solid pilots and successful implementations that contain actual cost and benefit metrics, as well as interorganizational pilots between trading partners — to identify further benefits and to explain how to overcome serious obstacles to full implementation. We will deal with this issue in a later chapter in which we prescribe a pilot methodology intended to document actual costs and benefits. The challenges, however, are not viewed as showstoppers, only bumps in the road. The hurdles continue to be scaled as understanding of what is actually involved increases.

But hurdles remain. Rajit Gadh writes a column for *Computerworld* through which he offers sound advice on mastering the complexities of RFID technology. According to Gadh, there is much more to the application than just slapping RFID tags on pallets and cases and shipping them. He advises: "The mandates are forcing product suppliers into accepting solutions from their technology providers that may not be ready for scalable deployment." As there is compliance, and suppliers absorb the early costs, however, Gadh sees a time when additional benefits might arrive and provide a justifiable return on investment. "The excitement of RFID is due to its ability to keep track of any product from cradle to grave as it moves through the various stages of its supply chain" (Gadh 2004).

CASE EXAMPLES SHOW THE POSSIBILITIES

There have been a number of success stories that provide incentive to the RFID movement, and they are not from the typical manufacturer to retail supply chain.

Consider first the case, reported by John Edwards for CXO Media, Inc. It seems the airlines have been trying to deal with a common but little known problem for years. As passengers, we take those carts that are used to move beverages and snacks up and down the aisles of airplanes for granted, as part of the equipment necessary for airline travel. But those carts can cost as much as $1,000 each. Tony Naylor, VP for in-flight solutions at eLSG.SkyChefs, an Irving, Texas–based supplier for the airline catering industry, reports on horrific stories "of airlines losing up to 1,500 carts in three months."

For this company, finding a solution went through investigation of RFID and a lot of subsequent work and due diligence. "It really was a bit of a minefield as we went through this because there were so many conflicting stories and opinions," Naylor advises. The company eventually selected Scanpak, a Dorval, Quebec–based company that offers Galley Equipment Tracking Systems, an RFID application targeted specifically at trolley management. The approach, of course, is to track the missing carts and get them returned to service (Edwards 2003).

The National Cattlemen's Beef Association (NCBA) is also fostering an RFID project intended to keep track of livestock at hundreds of thousands of ranches throughout the United States. Spurred by such buyers as Wal-Mart and McDonald's, interested in assuring high quality and no transmission of disease, the NCBA's program was launched in January 2004. A previous effort launched by the U.S. Department of Agriculture in December 2003 never fully materialized, although some states did have a measure of success.

There is serious motivation behind the current initiative, however, according to Kevin McGrath, president and CEO at Digital Angel Corporation, a supplier of tags to the industry. "The amount of money companies such as Wal-Mart and McDonald's could lose dwarfs the costs to implement a national identification program," McGrath states. And how big is the challenge? "There are at least 100 million cattle in the United States to chip and there are about 40 million slaughtered every year," he adds (Sullivan 2004b).

General Electric is known for its appliances and jet engines. The firm also has a very successful power plant systems division. In 2002, this division launched a project to attach active RFID tags to thousands of supplies, with an intent to track movement of all supplies. Nearly all suppliers have complied with this lesser known mandate. There are dual benefits from this effort. The suppliers have found they can move products through customs much faster and inventories at large job sites are kept for less time. This was not a forced mandate.

According to Sean Carney, program manager for Smart Asset Management at GE's $20 billion division, "We took the initiative to make this voluntary."

GE absorbed costs for suppliers, providing them with the active tags, which GE has determined can be recycled, erasing data stored on them. The benefits? According to Tahir Hamid, general manager of GE's power-plant systems, "Losing even one day can have a big impact on a power-plant project" (Bacheldor 2003a).

Other interesting developments include:

- Hospitals could use the technology to allow nurses to scan drugs at a patient's bedside and receive alerts if the wrong medication is being administered.
- Experiments are being conducted through which a warehouse or store could be scanned to instantly determine the contents.
- Getting rid of bad data can have a big payoff. Procter & Gamble decided to purge bad information that was being passed on to trading partners. During a subsequent data-cleansing process (a crucial step in complying with standards requirements), "P&G found thousands of redundancies in product description information, as well as data on products it doesn't sell anymore. Cleaning up data in one product-image database alone saved $1 million in fees related to maintaining those images," according to CIO Steve David (Hayes 2003, p. 32).
- Microsoft's home and entertainment division began shipping to Wal-Mart RFID-tagged cases and pallets containing Xboxes, computer games, software, keyboards, and mice. Microsoft has also begun to build RFID capabilities into its Navision and Axapta applications (Sullivan 2005a, p. 28).
- Hitachi and the European Central Bank have discussed using the "Mu-Chip," an RFID tag the size of a grain of sand incorporated into euro bank notes, to stem counterfeiting, to authenticate notes, and to automate counting (Collins 2003).

THE ROAD AHEAD

To say that the RFID movement has a long road ahead is to trivialize the amount of effort that needs to go into analyzing, documenting, and understanding the costs and benefits that are possible with this technology. While the initial mandated push for high-volume, pallet-level tagging is identifying a number of technological, environmental, and social hurdles that must be overcome, we expect to see numerous solutions appear in the next 24 months. Since the availability of the kind of data possible with an RFID system has not been available in the past, much work needs to be accomplished with interacting supply chains to develop the right applications, so the benefits will exceed costs. No doubt there will be a learning curve, along which the manufacturers and suppliers will bear the burden of cost, much as they would for a significant new technology development project.

Due to the expected amount of experimentation and subsequent learning that will be derived during the next two-year cycle, large organizations should be establishing a central source to stay current on happenings and to advise their businesses of the promises and problems. This technique avoids the need for multiple business units to spend test money to capture information and interpret results. Businesses should also select a single entity for pilot testing, using the results as a framework for further implementation.

There is another and larger factor to consider as the new roadway is constructed. As we have presented our case for RFID, we have positioned the technology as just one tool in the drive for full visibility into a supply chain, and ultimately one part of the future wireless business world. But what about RFID being a part of visibility into a lifeline? Consider what is happening at the Erlanger Medical Center in Chattanooga, Tennessee. In several of the facilities at that center, recessed antennas have been installed in the ceiling tiles, as part of a system intended to save the nurses time by allowing them to enter patient data wirelessly. According to John Haltron, Erlanger's network director, "This wireless technology is a foundation to a revolution in how we look at traditional patient care."

With rolling medical workstations, nurses can check vital signs and enter data electronically, in a paperless environment without errors. Lab results can be entered as well. Scanners facilitate dispensing prescriptions and medication, and the nurses can use Voice over Internet Protocol capabilities to respond to call button notices from anywhere in the center. The mobile nature of health care is a reason why facilities such as Erlanger are pursuing wireless technology and handheld computers, all part of the kind of new systems we see dotting the future landscape.

Haltron envisions hospitals "using the technology to track medical gear that's wheeled from room to room — like the 600 intravenous pumps that need periodic testing — by tagging them with RFID tags. Combine that with a wireless technology and a geographic information system at centralized monitoring areas, and a missing baby could be located immediately" (McGee 2003). This case is just one of a growing number that illustrate the potential of using RFID as a central tool in what is a much broader visibility system enhanced in a wireless environment.

SUMMARY

There can be little doubt that RFID technology is going to play a role in business and social transformation as processes are modified to include the use of wireless identification and tracking. Whether in a hospital, as part of a military campaign, or transforming a business process, there is an inevitable move toward using the new technology as an intelligent step toward eliminating the mistakes and extra time required to follow a product's path in the typical manually intensive environment. When asked if the current hype is for real or a temporary phenomenon, we reply strongly that we are witnessing the forward progress of an unstoppable technology adoption. It requires careful consideration of the possibilities and considerably more testing to prove the hidden values.

We have discussed many applications across the business and health services world, as a sampling of where the movement is making positive progress. The complications have also been cited, but make no mistake — the train is moving and the need is to determine how to take the ride and have a reasonable return on the cost of investment, development, and deployment. In the following chapters, we will continue our exploration of just how to accomplish that task.

3

RFID IN SUPPLY CHAIN APPLICATIONS: INVESTMENTS AND BENEFITS

We have portrayed RFID as an important new tool, which has found its way into an inevitable technology adoption cycle that will impact a wide variety of supply chains in a variety of industries and businesses. In spite of the tremendous attention being paid to the RFID concept per se, we persist in positioning this tool as one part of a larger scheme — as a means to gain greater knowledge through visibility into a supply chain system and eventually as an important mechanism in the emerging world of wireless technology and communication. The legacy of RFID will be that it went beyond bar coding (a 25-year-old technology) and other identification systems, to allow business managers direct access to what was occurring across a full global supply chain system and then to communicate valuable knowledge electronically to network constituents. With that knowledge, all members of the network gain greater value from the technology application.

RETURNS ON INVESTMENT BEGIN WITH NEW EFFICIENCIES

We expect many of these values to derive as RFID has a significant impact on some of the remaining inefficiencies afflicting most industry supply chains. Reference to Figure 3.1 provides a brief overview of some of the business areas

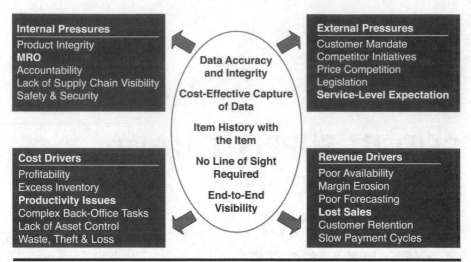

Figure 3.1. The Power of RFID: Business Results (Source: Rob Jackson, Computer Sciences Corporation)

to be impacted. Application of the technology should have an immediate and dramatic effect on the level of shrinkage and internal/external theft occurring in the retail sector and many delivery processes. Errors across the supply chain and the resulting need for reconciliation should drop as deployment expands and greater accuracy enters order processing and delivery. Associated Foods, a Utah wholesale distributor, found 125 people entering data at its main distribution center, and the information was wrong over 40 percent of the time. The inefficiencies in manufacturing and delivery will be improved as well, as firms learn how to use the technology to raise productivity. Companies involved in producing books and magazines, for example, report errors as the source of 35 percent of industry losses. One paper company has found in a study of forklift activity that the trucks are empty 60 percent of the time. All of these situations are targets for improvement with RFID. Administrative costs, in general, due to poor counts, bad pricing and terms, inaccurate identification, and other problems created by manual systems should drop with the use of RFID.

Nonsaleable goods resulting from damage, out-of-date products, and seasonal overstocks should also decrease. One report conducted by Timothy Jones, a professor at the University of Arizona, indicates that "40 percent to 50 percent of all food produced in the United States never gets eaten. Much of the waste is in the household, but the report reveals inefficiency in the supply chain. It says 26 percent of food in convenience stores and 10 percent of food in fast food restaurants goes to waste. The reason? The inability to match supply and demand" (Roberti 2005c).

For these and other reasons, we expect greater efficiency to be an attribute that will eventually bring more companies toward RFID applications. Conversely, in spite of the opportunities for serious improvements in almost every industry studied, we have been cautious to indicate that there are advocates and cynics at work, trying to drive acceptance and implementation forward in supply chains or attempting to stall and derail the RFID effort. In the face of much heated debate and the appearance of these separate camps, we propose to go forward and explain where we see the most immediate and successful area of execution: as a tool aiding visibility into supply chains. The counterpoint we develop will be built around understanding how RFID will eventually be a part of wireless technology, used in what becomes the network-connected digital supply chain.

Our hypothesis should be clear. RFID is not just a means of achieving compliant response for a few companies to a retail or military powerhouse that is forcing acceptance of the technology. It is a process rapidly becoming part of supply chain efforts through the work of a few pathfinders, aimed at taking advantage of the possibilities offered through automatic identification implementation. It will succeed as those on the forefront provide proof of concept and the larger body begins implementation not for the sake of dutiful compliance but to gain the potential business benefits. Only by having a return across the full supply chain network will RFID ever reach its full potential. In this chapter, supply chain applications will be outlined as we consider once again both sides of the controversy and develop our hypothesis and supporting arguments.

RFID AS AN ASSIST TO SUPPLY CHAIN

To begin, supply chains are no longer defined by simple linear process linkages, as illustrated in Figure 3.2. There was a time when this horizontal model connecting suppliers to manufacturing or production and on to storage and distribution to a retail outlet or facility for consumption was sufficient to diagram the system. The typical flows across such a system included the transfer of products and services, information, and finances. Most companies went to work to find best practices in all three areas. When there were difficulties, most companies simply added more inventory to the system to assure the minimum number of interruptions or outages. Support functions included information technology, communications accomplished through a local intranet, finance and

Support Functions: IT, Communications, Finance, HR

| Supplier | Inbound Logistics | Manufacturing | Outbound Logistics | Distribution Center | Retail Store | Consumer |

Figure 3.2.   The Traditional View of Supply Chain

accounting, and human resources. That was a simpler time than what exists today.

With the attention given to the actual end-to-end processing that takes place across most supply chains, and the extension of many supply chains to include offshore suppliers and customers, more complex models have made their appearance. Figure 3.3 more likely describes what has become the look of modern supply chains — a form of collaborative networks. Where a firm might have had a reduced supplier base bringing raw materials and parts downstream into

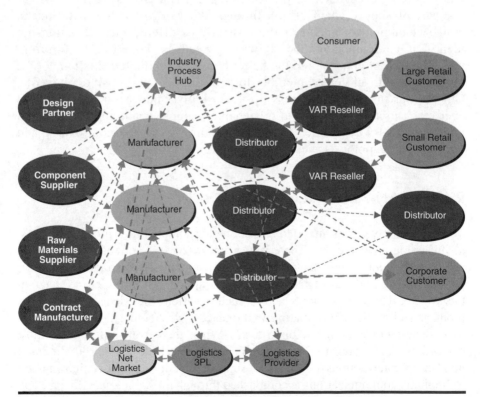

Figure 3.3.   Supply Chains Are Becoming Collaborative Networks

the manufacturing process, there are now echelons of supply, including the typical materials suppliers, but also contract manufacturers and suppliers of components and subassemblies. The manufacturer itself could have a series of other manufacturers, including competing firms, with which it secures other assemblies or to which it subcontracts a part of the finishing process. Boeing offers an example here, where it has made the decision to have major parts of its new 7E7 manufactured by Japanese and European sources. General Electric now sources part of its line of appliances from German manufacturer Bosch.

Design partners are now included to help bring the latest ideas and concepts into play and to shorten the cycle time from innovation to commercial acceptance. Procter & Gamble and Kraft Foods work with such a series of helpers to assure a steady stream of successful new products going through their supply chains. Hewlett-Packard has a global network of constituents working to bring new printers with superior features into the market in ever-decreasing time frames. The automobile firms have increasingly allowed first-tier suppliers to design parts of new cars.

Storage and transportation can move through a series of logistics providers, as an army of organizations have appeared, ready to store or transport part or all of a shipment. Distributors play a vital role in reaching specific market segments or establishing a niche position for certain market segments. SYSCO stands out as such a distributor, taking food products to a wide variety of institutions and feeding facilities, through a very sophisticated and effective redistribution delivery system. Identifying exactly what moves through such a system offers strong and immediate rewards for RFID technology deployment.

Value-added resellers could perform another step in the processing, especially for high-technology products and communication equipment. Amazon.com has gone from selling books to becoming an intermediary in the supply of appliances and electronic equipment through Best Buy and a host of other products delivered through an ever-growing number of business allies. Finally, the customer base has enlarged and been segmented into categories. Most supply chains now have separate channels of distribution to bring customized products and solutions to specific segments. The new marketing game is to have an abundance of information on each segment of importance, so demand can be generated, controlled, and matched accurately with supply. Looking backwards, today's consumer has a wide array of choices in terms of how he or she wants to purchase products and through which channel they should be delivered. The new game is to distinguish the ability of the supply chain network in the eyes of the most desirable customers and consumers.

The modern supply chain has indeed become a network of interacting constituents, each performing its critical process step and each needing as much data and knowledge as possible to ensure accuracy, timeliness, and effective performance. It is in this new world that RFID will find its greatest advantages — as a tool assisting the visibility into what is happening and a mechanism or catalyst for enabling the data transfer necessary to reach optimized conditions. Along each process step and through the handoff to other parties, RFID can provide the vital information on what is being moved and transferred and allow tracking from beginning to end of the total supply chain processing. RFID, when coupled to sensor networks, can also provide valuable information about the condition of assets. For example, food spoilage due to high temperature (or too low temperature) can be monitored and avoided. Alerts when high humidity conditions are present can save valuable electronic components in transit. Essentially this type of RFID sensor-based network can provide the visibility and chain of custody that can preserve product integrity.

RFID continues to gain acceptance in this environment, in spite of some strong opposition, as an enabler for those seeking visibility and supply chain optimization across a complex business network. In particular, the convergence of mandated initiatives, willing compliance, advancements in technology and components, and supporting standards is bringing the effort into focus as an important tool in global supply chain implementations. In that sense, it is being used to link companies and components from the point of need (store shelves, consumer homes) through the appropriate channel of supply and further upstream to the primary suppliers to those channels. It becomes a key enabler in the transfer of information across links, each of which needs what precedes and follows in order to effectively respond to what is happening.

COMPLEX DATA TRANSFER IS ENABLED

Figure 3.4 is a representation showing the relationships involved in a typical supply chain system between a consumer product manufacturer and a retailer. It shows that the connected supply chain relies on pertinent feedback and access to real-time information to coordinate activities across the extended enterprise displayed. Working in the manner that should be observed — from consumption upstream to the points of supply and replenishment — the diagram starts with collection of sales information, so the system knows what is being consumed and, therefore, what is in current demand. Point-of-sale (POS) data is the first link here, as a means of identifying current demand and what needs to be replenished and reflecting the correct information to those in inventory management across the network. This data moves to a retail headquarters environment for analysis and transfer to the suppliers. Note the additional services and constituents that could be involved as this knowledge moves toward the supplier, in an attempt to garner the most benefit from this knowledge.

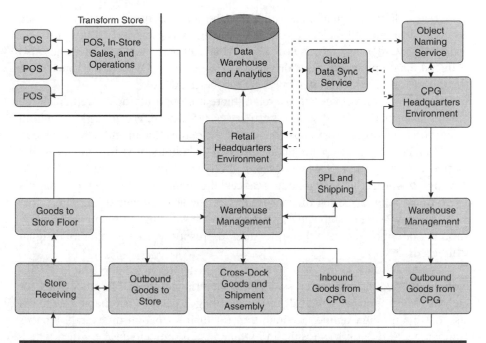

Figure 3.4. Overview of a Manufacturing-Retail Supply Chain (Source: Intel Corporation)

Consider, for example, a shoe manufacturer that wants to track what is occurring and keep retail stores stocked with the best-selling items. Currently, that consumer goods manufacturer has a system in place to relay POS information or current purchase orders back to a central processing center. At that location, current market information can be combined with near-term and long-term planning to adjust the system and make appropriate responses. The introduction of a new version of, say, a hot-selling sports shoe endorsed by a popular sports figure can be used to adjust manufacturing and delivery schedules. The same could happen with an especially popular cosmetic or perfume being manufactured by a branded firm and promoted by a celebrity. With RFID on a pallet basis, tracking across the system becomes better, but when the tags reach the individual shoe box or bottle of cologne, the firm will have data by gender, size, color, and so forth.

The cost of such an enabling system does not have to be extremely large. Procter & Gamble installed an RFID system in a manufacturing facility in Spain that involved RFID readers on forklifts and tags on the pallets for under $100,000, including equipment and installation. As the driver moves a truck through a warehouse door, a signal is delivered that the load is correct or incorrect. The system has increased factory throughput in what was previously a fully utilized warehouse. Order accuracy is now reported at 100 percent. The system has also reduced the number of forklift drivers by one per shift. Overall, the time frame for return on investment was one year (Roberti 2005c).

As the data moves further upstream, there are opportunities to replenish the goods taken out of the system with releases from an intermediate distribution center or a third-party warehouse operation. Here the shoe manufacturer can add RFID data to get a complete picture of what is being stored in regional distribution centers, company warehouses, and any third-party storage facilities. At the point where the information reaches the consumer product company's operations, another series of connections is made upstream to suppliers that need to know what to ship and downstream to the stores awaiting replenishment. Goods start moving in either direction, in response to the planning signal delivered.

Again, another series of warehouses or distribution centers might be involved or used simply for cross-docking material to attain full truckloads for delivery. In a modern sense, all of these linkages need to be enabled as much as possible through online, accurate transfer of information on exactly what is happening. Anything less results in extraneous and redundant activities, which in turn creates a need for extra safety stock and inventory. In the worst case scenario, sales are lost simply because demanded product is not available. RFID comes onto the scene as a means to determine actual flows and minimize extra stocks moving through the system, especially those that are not currently in demand.

The overall purpose of the linkages illustrated is to transfer information from the POS as far upstream as necessary, to the constituents that need the knowledge in order to make a proper response, through whatever intermediate steps are required. A fully deployed solution to any such need consists of a linked set of constituents that complete the response in the most effective manner, with each link depending on the actions of the other to attain anything close to optimized results. Returning to our shoe manufacturer, think of a system that begins with raw materials in Sri Lanka or the Philippines and progresses to sewing in Taiwan and shipment to ports in Europe and North America. Knowing what is in the system on a real-time basis can be a crucial piece of information, as market conditions change and the favored sports figure chooses another shoe design or is replaced by another more popular personality. If the system can be quickly purged of what will be less popular SKUs and filled with what will almost instantly be in demand, revenues are optimized and obsolete inventories minimized.

When executed, the results can be impressive. Retail shelves will be kept filled with the goods most in demand, and out-of-stocks disappear. Manufacturers will have the right parts for their assemblies, and distributors will be bringing what matches demand through the delivery system. This condition becomes possible because the movement of goods in response to the demand signal is tracked, an element of real-time control enters the supply chain picture, and inventories do not sink into a black hole. Currently, the cost of such an RFID-enabled system is beyond what provides an adequate return on investment for most applications, but as the technology improves, costs are reduced and greater scale is attained across many industries through discovery of more benefits, the returns will arrive.

Throughout the supply chain, the greatest gains come from improvements to process steps that result from better coordination and collaboration between the linked constituents. This is where the need for visibility, not just into the transfers but to improve the accuracy at the points where inventory is held and where sales are entered, becomes apparent. There is another need for such information as a support to special sales events, promotions, and new product introductions. Potential benefits include:

- Allowing the supply chain constituents to collaborate on purchasing activities and shipping instructions and tracking across the total network — taking advantage of network synergies
- Keeping inventory and stocking levels coordinated and connected to actual demand signals and changes in sales trends — matching supply with demand
- Improving decision making by identifying and analyzing changes and new buying patterns — so better responses are generated to meet what the data are actually saying
- Fine-tuning supply and sales activities based on accurate knowledge about product availabilities and current shipment schedules — avoiding the typical missteps that plague supply chains

VISIBILITY BECOMES THE DIFFERENTIATING FACTOR

In summary, the greatest enhancement from RFID to the total processing that occurs across a supply chain comes through having direct access and visibility into the end-to-end linkage, so the viewer can determine with far greater accuracy what is transpiring. Under such a condition, supply is matched in a much better manner with actual demand, and the flows are coordinated and synchronized with the most current needs foisted on the network by environmental or market conditions. Efficiency, customer satisfaction, and profitability rise under these conditions. To elaborate, consider some of the needed connections in a typical supply chain, as we use the actual flow of knowledge so important to effective supply chain response.

The POS data become product and store consumption information, a reflection of actual demand. The retailer's enterprise resource planning (ERP) and collaborative planning, forecasting, and replenishment (CPFR) systems come into play as real-time planning data are passed on to other constituents for entering into their ERP and CPFR databases. Data enter such systems now from a variety of sources that record actual sales and planning activities. Bar codes are scanned and data captured in store databases. Inventory movements are recorded through whatever facilities work in process or finished goods moved. How much better would all of this data gathering be if it were captured in real time and accurately traced without corruption, wherever it moved? The answer — to be provided through future pilot tests and many more implementations — will build the case for acceptance, not the demands of a few mega-consumers.

Consider two scenarios. The first is a manufacturer of large appliances, items that are heavy and bulky and easily damaged, like refrigerators, stoves, and dishwashers. Having tags that indicate exactly what is being handled and shipped and recording any extra information that reduces the liability for damage adds significant value. The second is a jewelry processor, which is moving expensive gold and diamond products. Again, accurate tracking at the item level could have a serious payback for an RFID-based system, in terms of recovery of potential losses, as well as the reduced amount of labor expense associated with periodic cycle counts.

With RFID, an operational logistics feedback loop is established between the retailer and its warehouse operations. The consumer goods manufacturer creates a similar link with its warehouse and delivery operations. Through a potentially large number of sources, goods flow back to the warehouses and on to the floors of the stores. Advance Shipping Notices appear in this system, as do receiving acknowledgments and all shipping data, all of which can be enhanced with more accurate and timely information. If reconciliation is necessary, that process step can be accommodated, as can any reverse logistics involved in returns or repairs, with the system providing a quick and direct means of aid. RFID can be an enabler across such a complex communication system by assuring transfer of all pertinent information on all movements. Synchronization of supply and demand becomes the real deliverable in a supply chain world that becomes increasingly oriented to a digital environment.

THE CONNECTED SUPPLY CHAIN OPERATES IN A DIGITAL ENVIRONMENT

A decade ago, very few people had an e-mail address. Today, most of us have several. Around the world, e-mail penetration moves inexorably toward high penetration levels. The Internet has blossomed from a concept by Tim Berners-Lee into an indispensable communication system. Where is it all headed? We see a world in which communication is instant and far reaching, not through copper wires or even fiber optic connections but through small handheld devices that send wireless messages to any business partner in a supply chain network. Mobile devices have already changed how most people conduct business by reaching remote constituents across extended enterprises.

The true role of RFID is expanded in this world, as we realize that modern supply chains must rely on instant transfer of accurate knowledge as markets begin transitioning from improved supply chain planning to better supply chain execution. That means an advanced supply chain is operating in a digital environment, using RFID as a tool to assure visibility into what is happening and as a means of transferring instant data about product movement. New areas of importance appear in this environment, establishing factors that can be critical to contemporary logistics and supply chain fulfillment. Among these factors, we would cite the following:

- Import and export documentation and compliance, which includes a landed cost analysis, tracking of multimodal shipments, and accurate settlement of all financial obligations
- Visibility and event management to monitor inventory status and movements throughout the extended supply chain network and track actual changes in real time
- Details of constituent responsibility, including any third-party sourcing or transportation services, structure and cost of relationships, measurement, and compliance rules
- Management of the transactions that take place, including any load changes, shipment transfers, and routing or scheduling changes
- Management of any return movements, repairs, or restoration of goods and the resolution of materials moved to stock or disposal

Metro Group AG, Germany's top retailer, has taken a definite step in that direction. The firm is testing RFID in its warehouse management system, to enable automatic inspection of incoming goods at its showcase "Future Store" in Rheinberg. Goods delivered to this store "are fitted with RFID tags in the central warehouse and read upon arrival at the store." During transportation from the warehouse to the sales floor, "goods are read again, and identified as items to be moved to the front of the store. The tests in Rheinberg have shown that RFID offers retailers and their customers enormous advantages: more effective processes, less out-of-stocks and subsequently lower costs, which benefit both parties." With RFID, goods can be located along the entire supply chain — from production to the shelf in the store (Foster 2004, p. 36).

We can take a different look at what one of the key drivers behind the RFID effort is doing to see where the future will evolve. Wal-Mart is not just pursuing RFID as an identification device. It wants that technology to be a part of voice-directed work, in warehouses, distributions centers, and even on the store floor. Consider the description depicted in Figure 3.5. Here we see that the giant retailer is using information technology to integrate its entire supply chain. From suppliers to stores, the goods and information related to those goods are tracked through an end-to-end network system that includes satellite communication. Day-to-day sales data secured at the point of purchase (cash registers)

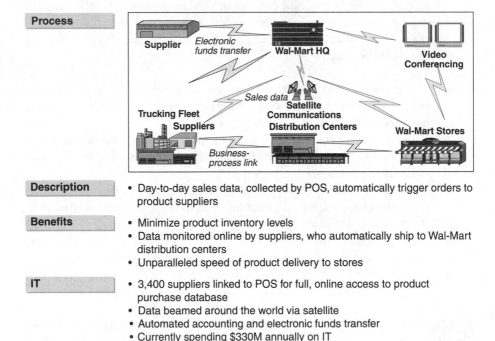

Description
- Day-to-day sales data, collected by POS, automatically trigger orders to product suppliers

Benefits
- Minimize product inventory levels
- Data monitored online by suppliers, who automatically ship to Wal-Mart distribution centers
- Unparalleled speed of product delivery to stores

IT
- 3,400 suppliers linked to POS for full, online access to product purchase database
- Data beamed around the world via satellite
- Automated accounting and electronic funds transfer
- Currently spending $330M annually on IT

Figure 3.5   Wal-Mart Uses Information Technology to Integrate the Entire Supply Chain, from Production to Store Shelf, Based on Real-Time Information

are collected and automatically used to trigger new orders to the product suppliers. Wal-Mart has 3,400 suppliers already linked to its POS system, giving them full, online access to the firm's product purchase database. Included is an automated accounting and electronic funds transfer mechanism.

With this type of system as the benchmark, we expect to see further enhancements. Voice technology will eventually be used by warehouse and store managers to enable labor-intensive functions, including receiving, storing, order picking, and inventory management. Look for the talking warehouse and delivery system to be a part of forthcoming warehouse management and transportation management systems — in fact, through the use of RFID on your products, your inventory will talk to you.

In some regards, just as we thought about and managed our supply chains in a linear fashion decades ago, we are applying the same linear thinking to RFID-enabled processes. Certainly, RFID has the potential to provide an unprecedented amount of detail-level information in real time. The greater question becomes: How will this enormous amount of knowledge be managed? What new business processes will RFID enable and what processes will be reduced or eliminated? Most importantly, how will RFID make an organization more competitive and increase its profitability?

The answers to these questions can be found by viewing RFID as future visibility on display, in the context of wireless information gathering and sharing, enhancing the speed and details of product dates. When viewed from this vantage point, RFID should be used as a tool that allows the accurate communication of at minimum three factors: identity, location, and time. With RFID as the monitoring system, your assets and inventory can speak to you. Through access to this information, visibility of raw material, work in process, finished goods, and real-time product usage or consumption is possible — at whatever granular level is relevant for the efficient operation of the business. Now you can "act on fact" rather than rely on formula or forecasts.

RFID BECOMES A VISIBILITY-ENABLING TOOL

RFID becomes an excellent tool to power this visibility, but as an enabling technology it must work in seamless concert with existing product-tracking applications and the infrastructure of the organization. We outlined our model for RFID adoption in Chapter 1. The key to applying that model is the understanding that RFID is not a solution unto itself. The real value and real breakthroughs in business process transformation will arrive when RFID is used appropriately to shape, manage, and move knowledge amongst these processes and to create radically different business processes and business models.

For example, one of the objectives for Wal-Mart as part of its RFID mandate is to eliminate out-of-stocks at the shelf level. RFID at the case level can accomplish this task by providing real-time product movement (e.g., from distribution center to retail center back room to the sales floor) within Wal-Mart's supply chain. This becomes a case of using RFID to track and manage product movement in order to improve product availability, thus improving revenue growth and customer satisfaction, by reducing lost sales — a chronic retail problem being attacked by a variety of new technologies. Eventually, when confidence in RFID improves, experience grows, and costs of implementation decline, suppliers will be in position to move up the RFID adoption curve and view the retailer's shelf space as an extension of their own warehousing and delivery systems.

At this level of performance and visibility, new forms of payment for product will appear, among which are the following examples:

- Partial customer payments based on location and movements within the customer's supply chain. These terms could even be tied to velocity of product movement, ultimately replacing net 10 or net 30 terms. Suppliers would have an incentive in this scenario to aggressively monitor their product movement, working with the retailer to dynamically move and shift product based on real-time demand signals and real-time product availability alerts.

- While suppliers currently pay a premium for preferred shelf space and product location, with RFID at the item level suppliers will now have a visibility tool to ensure that their product is in fact in the preferential location.

- Taking the shelf space example further, suppliers that use specially designed product displays tied to new product introductions or product promotions should investigate the capabilities of intelligent shelf displays that would ensure product is maintained by the retailer throughout the promotion period. The trade-off in increased investment in this type of intelligent promotional display may be outweighed by the reduction in out-of-stocks.

Our vision of the future includes a ubiquitous environment in which advanced supply chain systems are linked into a network of communication, transferring digital information through a linked series of wireless devices. In this state, there is full connectivity across the critical business partners, so end-to-end visibility is not a concept but a reality. Access to the actual business conditions everywhere in the network at the same time is at the heart of optimizing the processing that takes place. Telephones, laptop computers, and cameras are already progressing toward such an environment and will be used as enablers to the wireless systems we contemplate. RFID plays well in this scenario, as it provides a direct and wireless link to the necessary data on product location and flow.

Consider how special marketing efforts and event management can be enabled as actual consumption knowledge is transferred in a ubiquitous environment; search-related advertising becomes a tool that consumers use rather than despise. In Figure 3.6, we see supply chain visibility described in three layers. Internal integration begins at the bottom, with three systems: purchasing, logistics planning, and order management. This information is brought together and then transferred into the event management level or special effort area, via the Internet. Now a repository is created for accessing what data are available that have an effect on the circumstances surrounding the event. The third level is reached when the necessary knowledge of what is happening is transferred for external integration and all of the key supply chain constituents receive real-time information on what is transpiring.

Several advantages begin to occur. The constituents, including those normally left out of the knowledge loop (second-tier suppliers, distributors), gain information about the status of movements and inventory. Through the repository, the players retain and can summarize historical trends in the data for future

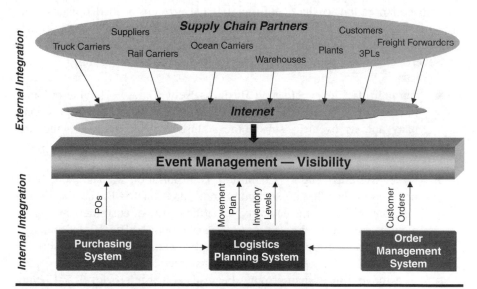

Figure 3.6. Supply Chain Visibility Has Three Levels

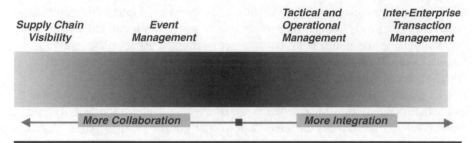

Figure 3.7. Spectrum of Supply Chain Execution Systems

reference or application. With RFID enablement, this information is far more accurate and displayed in real time. As significant trends are observed or innovative responses developed to what the data are showing, supply chain partners can share these insights and establish a collaborative platform for getting more from future events.

This type of advanced supply chain involvement is just the beginning. Such collaboration creates a spectrum of supply chain execution systems, as illustrated in Figure 3.7. The importance of this spectrum will be described in greater detail in Chapter 7, where we consider RFID in the retail sector. What can be seen is that as a company and its business allies move across the spectrum, they gain visibility of product that is moving or at rest within the total supply chain through collaboration to share information and provide needed updates. The movement toward tactical, operational, and interenterprise management becomes easier through the integration of constituents' systems.

Several examples point the way toward the world we envision:

- Through its Global Samsung Business Network, a worldwide collaborative portal communication system, the Korean-based electronics company and its overseas subsidiaries, close business partners, and key customers have a real-time view of the status of purchase orders, sales, shipping, and inventory.
- Ryder Systems' Supply Chain and Transportation Management Solutions group handles all outbound transportation for Bacardi's Florida distribution center. Instead of being at the mercy of customers arranging pickups, due to consignees controlling outbound traffic, Ryder manages the processing using digital data through a web-based solution available to Bacardi personnel, carriers, and customers.
- In a move aimed at improving beer sales at a micro level, 7-Eleven, the convenience store leader, installed a digital operating system using

sales and demand data to predict shifting preferences from multiple packs to single units. An entire line of low-carbohydrate products was also introduced through what emerged as the firm's "Team Merchandising" program, enabled through timely and accurate information on consumption.

■ Three years after the 9/11 terrorist attacks, cargo container security remains a key issue for importers and exporters. Improvements have been made. Carriers now electronically transmit information on carrier contents to the U.S. Customs Automated Manifest System, with a full description of all contents. Web-enabled video, RFID devices, global positioning system tracking, and supporting software are all parts of the eventual total container security effort — another example of what can occur in the new environment.

CONCLUSIONS

So what are the markets and opportunities for RFID in our brave new world of supply chain? Improved, granular-level tracking and tracing will be greatly enabled. As the technology and standards are further developed, use will expand and costs will decline. Emerging markets will be considered in later chapters, including aerospace and defense, pharmaceuticals and health care, consumer goods and retail, and others. Watch the U.S. Food and Drug Administration use the technology to ensure quality control and eliminate the gray and black markets for pharmaceutical products. The costs will be large in the beginning, but the savings will eventually match and exceed the investments.

This condition is in fact the key challenge confronting RFID at the moment. Many would-be suppliers faced with the burden of full compliance consider their initial investments in RFID as sunk out-of-pocket costs, no-return trials, and throwaway investments. The catch-22 is that many of these same suppliers do not disagree with the vision offered by RFID. If meaningful progress is to be made, they must begin investing now in order to capture the later business values. Timing, scope, and scale of RFID investigation are critical elements for successful project management and risk minimization.

Supply chain benefits will eventually come from eliminating loss of revenue through out-of-stock conditions and the saving of assets (lives, from the military and medical viewpoint). There will be improvements and savings with put-away and picking systems, along with generally improved asset tracking. Customer satisfaction can be expected to increase when the right goods are always in the right place at the right time. Deductions taken for misshipments will be eliminated. Labor associated with locating misplaced inventory and heroic expediting will be greatly reduced. Returns and recall processes should diminish in magnitude and importance. There will be a time when we see reduced handling and lower shrinkage and automated receipt and reorder. Holding of slow and obsolete inventory will be a thing of the past. These and more benefits will be explained as we now move from our generalized view of RFID in supply chain to areas of specific interest.

4

RFID STRATEGY AND IMPLICATIONS FOR A BUSINESS

We have been portraying the conflict surrounding acceptance or rejection of radio frequency identification in supply chains, taking care to point out arguments from both the advocacy and cynical camps. When a clearer picture of what is involved is mastered, and after a reasonable period of gestation, a company must make a decision on which course to accept and then build a definition of its RFID business posture into its strategic plan. We see a shortening of the time in which the decision can be forestalled, although some cynics are suggesting it is over a decade long. Forward and reverse are the possible directions, but a choice must be made and a strategy developed.

To aid the decision makers, we have promoted RFID as a tool in supply chain visibility and in a wireless technology business environment. With so many constituents seeking information in a contemporary supply chain, increased visibility in a real-time format has become essential. With communication across such an elaborate network also moving inexorably toward a wireless system, we again see a position for RFID to enhance the collaborative possibilities.

From both the positive and negative aspects, we will continue to consider how a firm involved in a supply chain and subsequently as part of an extended enterprise will find important applications for RFID, recognizing that some organizations will wait passively on the sidelines as the scenario plays out. Since we view the development as an inevitable trend, however, it is important that we position acceptance or rejection within a strategic framework.

Whether as a supplier, manufacturer, distributor, or retailer, the promises and problems surrounding RFID must be translated into a definite business strategy and operating plan — either endorsing or resisting the movement. With so much initial investment involved, this move cannot be made casually, although some firms are doing so just to meet the mandates they have received. For those firms determined to go forward, RFID implementation should be part of a controlled risk effort, within a coherent strategy that defines the position and applications for the technology.

At the same time, RFID can no longer be considered as just an experiment in progress. Once the costs and benefits are better understood, and a strong case for action is developed and accepted by senior management, it must be translated as well into a marketing plan, with the applications defined and timetables for execution established — so benefits can be achieved and a reasonable return on investment can finally be generated. This chapter will follow the emerging work in the RFID movement and show how some companies are following a game plan that meets the current demands of the large buyers while developing a strategy to provide adequate returns on the RFID investment.

GETTING BEYOND THE MANDATES TO A SENSIBLE STRATEGY

It is one thing to try and satisfy the demands of extremely large buyers, which in some cases might make the difference between survival and failure of the firm. In such a situation, the means of controlling risk is to adopt a strategy that includes meeting minimum standards while keeping costs as low as possible. With the movement toward RFID picking up steam, such a position can only be short term in nature. The number of RFID projects grows on a daily basis. More stable and uniform standards are appearing around the corner. Heavyweights, like Cisco Systems, have jumped into the picture and should help reduce the costs of entry and participation. Cisco says "RFID fits neatly into its long-term strategy to build RFID into its routers, switches, and software" (Sullivan 2005a, p. 25).

Many retailers are becoming more familiar with the technology and moving forward on their installation plans. Ace Hardware Corporation has been testing RFID and plans to deploy the technology across its 15 distribution centers by the end of 2005. Ace has the dual need to improve its supply chain costs and help with the supply chain needs of independent hardware store owners and their consumers. The company believes RFID will provide an assist. With these and more stories hitting the daily news, the reasonable approach is to begin development of a substrategy to the current business plan, one that blends the RFID technology and use with existing strategies in a manner that controls the risk and prepares the firm to receive enough benefit to at least break even in the early stages, until a real return can be secured in the long term.

Developing such a strategy and positioning it within a supply chain effort will require attention to a number of important factors:

- Enumeration of the costs, delivery enhancements, potential savings, and effect on customer satisfaction that will be influenced by RFID applications — making at least an order-of-magnitude assessment of the costs and benefits involved with execution across an extended enterprise
- Definition of the steps necessary to execute a meaningful strategy for RFID and its relationship within the greater business strategy, operating plan, and supply chain model being pursued — explaining to key stakeholders what the firm plans to do and how it affects current business posture
- Exploration of piloting RFID-enabled processes with selected trading partners to identify shared benefits, instead of limiting RFID pilots to processes that take place within the "four walls" of the organization
- Listing the functions and services that acceptance and deployment of RFID can bring to the business and its supply chain strategy — identifying where value can be added beyond satisfying key customer mandates — including tactical and strategic issues
- Beginning documentation of the expected financial impact that will derive from an RFID deployment, starting with controlled experiments and pilot tests to provide meaningful metrics — getting your hands on what the future state might really look like and how it will affect profits

ENUMERATING POTENTIAL COSTS AND BENEFITS

E. & J. Gallo Winery offers an example of the first consideration, as this firm struggles with finding a sensible answer regarding deployment while faced with possibly conflicting needs. Gallo is pulled, on the one hand, by major retailers insisting on compliance and trying, on the other hand, to apply the RFID technology across its extensive distributor base. This California-based firm manages over 2,000 product SKUs in over 90 countries with 600 distributors/wholesalers. Gallo has been hard at work forging a plan for using RFID technology in its supply chain with an eye on both constituencies.

Since Gallo is among the roughly 200 second-wave consumer products companies required to ship its products to Wal-Mart stores with RFID tags on cases and pallets by a January 2006 deadline, the mandate is a partial driver behind action. To comply, Gallo is making a sizable initial investment and has set up a test project at its Modesto warehouse, where the firm is piloting compliance. Through this effort, the firm will most likely enhance its understanding of exactly what it will encounter as it moves forward along its path to compliance.

From another aspect, Gallo has an eye on some traditional supply chain issues in its business environment. Because of the particular requirements in its business, the wine maker needs to include its U.S. distributors in any Auto-ID picture, because state laws generally require that wine and spirits be sold to retailers through in-state distributors. Without the involvement of these distributors, the effort could be wasted. "This opens a discussion on who really owns the responsibility of the identification for the case and the mixed pallets," according to Ernie Chachere, Gallo's VP of supply chain. "There's a lot of discovery left to do," he states (Sullivan 2005a, p. 24). Gallo is well advised to use its pilot operation to determine what other costs and potential benefits might be involved as it completes its delivery of products through its necessary intermediaries. It can also use the experiment to determine the benefits or lack thereof to its vast distributor base.

Up to now, most suppliers and manufacturers have been keeping a close eye on the first wave of 137 Wal-Mart suppliers, committed to meeting a 2005 deadline. Large companies like Gillette, Procter & Gamble, and Unilever have already begun to ship pallets and cases to a number of Wal-Mart distribution centers in Texas, as part of the shorter term mandate. At the same time, German retailer Metro Group AG has gone further, with 20 suppliers shipping goods to 20 locations with RFID tags. Unfortunately, actual cost information is so far sparse at best. As these efforts continue to develop, a company caught in the web of compliance must enumerate the costs it will encounter, capture any potential savings it might find, determine how delivery might be enhanced, and postulate how the customer experience might be improved. This exercise begins with a rough estimate of start-up costs.

In our work, as of the publication of this book, we use the following budgetary figures (the low to high ranges are driven primarily by quantity, functionality, and feature) to determine an order of magnitude of the costs involved with RFID implementation:

- Passive RFID tags, passive 915-MHz Electronic Product Code (EPC) Gen 1 and 2 — $0.20 to $0.45 each

- RFID label printers (EPC Gen 1 or 2) — $5,000 to $8,000 each
- RFID high-speed label applicators — $15,000 to $25,000 each
- EPC-compliant antennas — $250 to $600 each
- EPC-compliant readers — $500 to $2,500 each

If a firm is planning its first pilot, in many cases purchasing a vendor's evaluation kit (which typically contains 100 tags, one reader, two antennas, power supply, data capture software, and associated cabling) for approximately $5,000 is a good first step. Also, in order to provide for reasonable budgetary estimates when calculating first-year deployment costs, we suggest using the higher end of the estimates provided above.

Estimating the cost of the middleware to commission, capture, and manage the data provided by RFID is perhaps the most difficult area at this time. Simple one- or two-point applications (where a read point would be one reader) can be run using the software that is delivered with the RFID label printer, such as those provided by Monarch/Paxar or Zebra Technologies. This software, when used with Microsoft Excel, is adequate for capturing and storing RFID tag data. If your deployment strategy calls for adding several read points over a short period of time, coupled with using multiple label printers, serious consideration should be given to using one of the RFID middleware packages designed for more extensive deployments. These applications range in price from $15,000 to $100,000 depending on functionality, number of instances installed, and degree of integration.

When considering the purchase of RFID middleware, attention needs to be given to what you want the middleware to accomplish. Middleware application functionality varies from the simple (commission and record EPC number assignment) to middleware that can manage EPC number assignment as well as manage your RFID hardware infrastructure to the more complex arrangements that provide integration into your enterprise resource planning system. Also, almost all warehouse management systems now include RFID as an extension of their current solution offering. Matching the data management requirements to your deployment schedule and degree of integration will help determine what type of middleware is appropriate for your organization.

STEPS TOWARD AN RFID STRATEGY

With a rough cut on the costs and benefits, Figure 4.1 can be used as a beginning point in the strategy development we are espousing. A company embarks with the understanding that the first step in developing a strategy that impacts supply

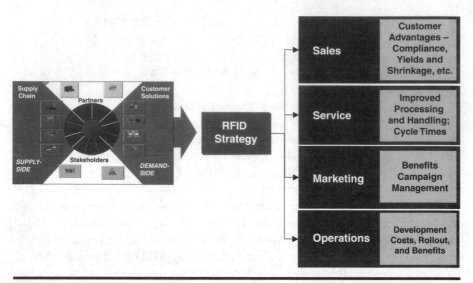

Figure 4.1. RFID Strategy Must Satisfy Stakeholder Needs: RFID Strategy Is Only a Part of the Greater Business and Supply Chain Strategy and Should Reflect the Impact on Key Elements of the Business

chain should define, confirm, and refine the common set of business require-ments that the firm must satisfy. The second step is to develop a conceptual framework depicting a possible improved future state. Figure 4.2 was drawn for a pharmaceutical manufacturer seeking an improved delivery system and used as the firm developed its RFID/supply chain strategy. The improved state, of course, can be far more detailed, but it should identify the product flows and inventories to be positively affected by the RFID technology.

From this information, again using Figure 4.1, the company should identify the key stakeholders to be impacted by adoption of the RFID technology and decide how success will be defined and measured. In many cases, these con-stituents will be similar to those previously affected by bar coding or other auto-ID systems. Starting on the demand side of the illustration, but eventually expanding to the supply side, the firm creates a list of the key areas to be considered, like those in the figure. Each part of the developing matrix should include pluses and minuses, as the analysis must provide an honest and frank evaluation of what adopting an RFID strategy will mean to the business and its important stakeholders.

For each of the constituents chosen, the resulting in-depth analysis should generate a point of view on what is intended to be accomplished and what the

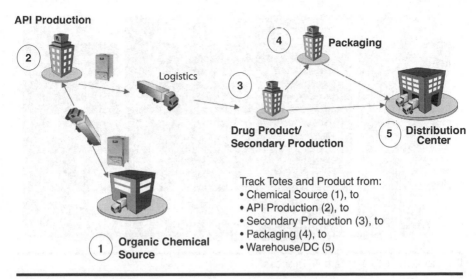

API Production

Figure 4.2. Pharmaceutical Manufacturer's World

basic implementation plan might include. Fitting any plan within the greater context of the overall company strategy and business plan will serve to assure these stakeholders that the adoption of RFID does not change the current business posture, but reinforces the basic tenets. Eventually, each of these stakeholders should find extra values as a return on the effort.

Figure 4.3 goes to the next step and illustrates the processes involved in forming a specific RFID strategy. It begins with a market analysis that reviews the industry imperatives, as understood at the moment and as anticipated in a near-term and long-term time frame. That should include the positives and negatives. A review of what competitors might be doing or planning should be included, with an assessment of what impacts can safely be anticipated from the technology adoption. A few of the most important customers and samples from other parts of the segmented customer base should be analyzed to develop a picture of the expected customer reaction. A projection of RFID hardware costs (tags, antennas, readers, etc.) must be made in order to understand at what point an acceptable return on investment can be achieved. Also, a survey of potential government regulations (e.g., food or pharmaceutical tracing) that could affect the business process of the organization must be incorporated as part of the strategy. Other factors of importance to a specific situation can be included, but the market analysis must reflect an honest assessment of what is going to be a part of the business future.

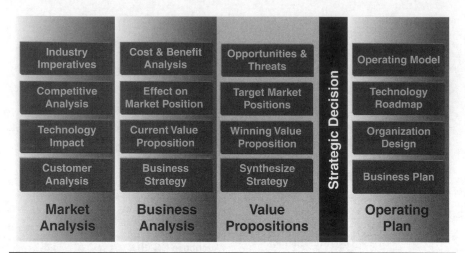

Market Analysis	Business Analysis	Value Propositions	Strategic Decision	Operating Plan
Industry Imperatives	Cost & Benefit Analysis	Opportunities & Threats		Operating Model
Competitive Analysis	Effect on Market Position	Target Market Positions		Technology Roadmap
Technology Impact	Current Value Proposition	Winning Value Proposition		Organization Design
Customer Analysis	Business Strategy	Synthesize Strategy		Business Plan

Figure 4.3. RFID Strategy Process

While this book contrasts the arguments for and against RFID adoption, our premise is that RFID will be an effective tool in supply chain management. Our recent experience has shown that any organization, whether it is under a mandate or not, should evaluate the potential benefits, opportunities, and challenges of RFID as part of its overall supply chain management strategy. In fact, a review of the case study material available to date indicates that early adopters are uncovering real bottom-line benefits from the use of RFID within their own operations and that further benefits arise when incorporating applications with their trading partners.

Every business seeking to resolve an RFID strategy needs to answer five critical questions here and for the balance of the strategy development process:

- How sustainable is the business or how much and what part might be at risk if RFID becomes an accepted business practice in our industry or market?
- How capable are our existing processes to accept the changes, meet the expected needs and demands of the market, and satisfy key customers with RFID as an enabler?
- What is the cost/benefit of noncompliance?
- How can the technology be used beyond compliance to enhance other processes within the supply chain?
- What is the best strategy to succeed and add value for all constituents?

The answers to these queries will help establish the background against which any decisions will be made. Now the second step in creating an RFID strategy is to develop a business analysis that applies the answers to the questions and begins to fit the emerging concepts with market conditions, without bankrupting the firm. In the business analysis sector of the process diagram, the firm starts with an outline of whatever is known about costs and benefits, drawing on what came out of the first step. Consideration must be given to the anticipated effect on market position of having or not having RFID capability. Then a look is given at the current value proposition being brought to the market to determine if it needs modification or, more correctly, how the RFID strategy can be successfully harmonized to appear as a logical extension of the current approach. Then the business strategy starts to unfold — as an extension of the current strategy and business plan.

When value propositions are considered, the effort moves to another level, and a deep and frank review is made of the opportunities and threats posed by adoption or rejection of the RFID technology. Now the firm considers target market positions and how the opportunities and threats will directly impact important segments. The hardest part of the exercise is to then develop winning value propositions that not only secure the desired market positions but provide a reasonable return on the effort. With these values in hand, the firm then synthesizes the strategy into sellable bullet points, understandable across the business, and begins co-development of an execution plan with key network constituents. Upon thorough review of what has been developed and most likely many iterations, a set of strategic decisions are then made to guide the rollout and deployment — hopefully through risk-mitigating pilots and test to prove the value of the chosen concepts.

Upon verification of these decisions through positive test results, a modified business plan is created, reflecting the new operating model (as an adaptation to the existing model), with a technology roadmap to guide implementation of the RFID strategy. Whatever changes are needed to organizational design are documented and explained, and a final business plan is blessed by all key stakeholders, so execution can begin in earnest. However, it is important to accept early in the planning process that this is a plan that must be constantly updated with new information gathered from pilot tests, proof-of-concepts, new RFID market data, customer requirements, and legislative activity.

Once the operating model has been developed, the firm should determine how the supply chain will be better enabled. That requirement sets up the need to document the enablement options, as described in a generalized case in Figure 4.4. Here we see many of the supply chain constituents arrayed against

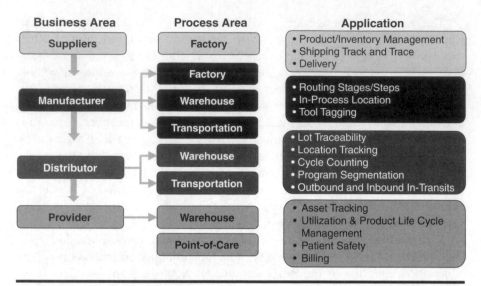

Figure 4.4. Document RFID Enablement

the affected process areas and some possible RFID applications. Again, this model must be customized for the specific firm and industry.

DOCUMENT VALUES TO BE ADDED WITH RFID

With so much controversy present, the advocates and cynics will be busy delivering opinions on the model and strategy, during the development process and as the final strategy is revealed. As a supplement to the previous step, the go-forward firm should begin listing the functions and services that an RFID deployment can bring to the business and how it will augment the supply chain strategy. We recommend beginning with the functions and process steps in the supply chain that will be most affected by having greater visibility. A review of the current process map for the business provides a valuable assist in this regard, from which the firm can select its starter kit of potential improvements. We like to include:

- **The customer order management process** — where RFID can improve the accuracy of incoming data and enhance the transfer of data from point to point
- **Inventory planning and management** — where RFID can result in the need for less inventories (raw materials, work in process, subparts, and

finished goods) by virtue of being able to quickly identify the quantity and location of all goods in the end-to-end supply chain network

- **Purchasing, procurement, and strategic sourcing** — through lower costs generated through less embedded scanning, locating, expediting, and tracking costs on the part of suppliers
- **Manufacturing, fabricating, and production** — because of lower handling costs, better tracking of supplies without calling for duplicates, and greater ability to perform under a kanban or advanced just-in-time delivery system
- **Warehousing and distribution** — with significantly lower cost to verify contents, locations, and availability of needed supplies and finished goods
- **Transportation management** — because of fewer emergency shipments, better cross-docking, and fuller loads by virtue of knowing exact locations and readiness for pickup
- **Customer response and calls for service** — through elimination of the bulk of requests to find missing products or to better match actual demand with what is in the supply chain
- **Customer billing and accounts payable** — to improve the speed of collections and to reduce some of the current deductions and invoice reconcilement process

As an example of the last function, consider an opportunity to use RFID to enable more accurate Advance Shipping Notices (ASNs), to reduce discrepancies and invoice deductions. According to one system analyst and supply chain expert, consumer products manufacturers lose as much as 10 percent of their total annual sales due to invoice deductions by retailers, with only about 14 percent being recovered. If that amount could be improved by half through revised ASN processes, these manufacturers could regain three-quarters of a point of profit on the bottom line — in addition to savings in operations and customer service.

One expert, Joe McKinney, advises: "Even manufacturers choosing a 'slap and ship' strategy for RFID compliance can attack the [invoice deduction] problem by RFID-enabling one door shipping to the RFID-requesting retailer. By providing a point of shipment ASN to their customers, rather than a picklist based ASN, and by requiring a matching point of receipt proof of delivery from their customers, manufacturers drive up ASN accuracy while driving down invoice deductions" (McKinney 2005, p. 29).

It should be kept in mind that the RFID technology field is still in a development stage, and new innovations and ideas will mold its eventual full capability, the benefits of which may be hard to initially define. As implementation grows, some very interesting applications appear. NASA has completed a successful test of RFID tags as part of an effort to create a real-time network that "would continuously monitor hazardous chemicals stored in five National Aeronautics and Space Administration facilities at Edwards Air Force Base in Southern California." The purpose is to "detect and react to break-ins, chemical thefts, and dangerous spills" (Sullivan 2005b).

On occasion, a strategy will move forward without the traditional clear return on investment. However, couldn't such a system be used by any organization that needs to monitor, manage, and report the status of OSIIA-designated hazardous chemicals in use within its own operations? Couldn't a case for return on investment be made by improving worker safety and reducing insurance liability? Answers to these queries broaden the scope for finding returns on the effort.

RFID-powered global networks continue to take shape as well. The U.S. Department of Defense (DOD) is deploying such a system to capture benefits in its supply chain, which will be described in Chapter 6. RFID has already been credited with saving DOD "$300 to $500 million, reducing required support containers by 90% and shortening critical supply cycle time in the current Operation Iraqi Freedom campaign." The federal agency will continue to use bar codes, but views "RFID as a critical enabling technology for DOD Logistics Transformation, a program to facilitate hands-free capture for an integrated DOD supply chain enterprise" (Sarma 2005, p. 1).

From a general viewpoint, among the more obvious potential values to be brought to these functions and services, we suggest:

- Definition of what values can be added to core competencies that will result in sustained or increased revenues and enhancements to desired supply chain results — such as visibility into the processing so goods can be identified anywhere in the supply chain and duplicate or redundant steps or inventories avoided and customers no longer guess at what is being delivered and can make changes without disrupting the supply chain.
- Alignment of the supply chain effort, using RFID as an enabler with the company's business objectives — so the key customers do not feel threatened during the transformation and develop additional backup sources of supply. By sensing the change as an extension of previously successful systems of identification and response rather than a potentially irresponsible gamble, most customers will exhibit more patience during the inevitable ramp-up curve of execution.
- Establishment of a consistent communication message that drives successful implementation and elicits further development of payback fea-

tures, by making everyone aware of the strategy, expected impacts, timetables, and elements of risk. In that way, each party affected can do its planning as well, with the understanding of what might or might not develop as deliverables.

■ Reduction of any potential gaps in expected performance that could radically erode market position or put the firm at risk versus more adept competitors. Since the effort is not going away, the firm is well advised to create a strategy and get it tested, so any shortcomings are quickly addressed and removed.

■ Development of a go-forward framework or roadmap that will minimize the inherent risks and eventually justify the trip — completed through enough actual pilots, tests, and direct experiences to show the actual costs and benefits and a roadmap to a successful future state.

At a more generic level, some of the reasons that support becoming involved with RFID include:

■ Improved return on assets and capital employed through less working capital tied up in obsolete or redundant inventories

■ Facilitation of product recall and traceability of damaged or disputed goods

■ Increased asset accuracy through the presence of an invisible asset tag that is permanent

■ Reduced data capture labor and back office functions

■ Improved planning and delivery systems enabled through more accurate real-time data

■ Improved compliance to Sarbanes-Oxley reporting requirements

BUILD A FINANCIAL CASE FOR ACTION

The next step is to go beyond order-of-magnitude cost and benefit estimates, and the estimated benefits described, to develop an actual financial case for action. The question being answered at this point is: Why are we going through the proposed set of activities supporting this RFID strategy? The answer must provide a reason for developing, selling, and delivering an RFID-based solution or system to customers — those demanding compliance and those unsure of the overall benefits. Where costs are still unknown and new technologies expected to have an impact, reliable ranges can be used, but the purpose is to document what will be encountered, so the risks can be evaluated and kept under control. Pilots and tests, of course, can be a part of this effort, as the mysterious becomes more concrete.

During this part of the effort, the focus should be kept on business process improvement rather than technology, using the former to get the processing correct and the latter to enhance the processing. As the RFID strategy progresses and alignment around its concepts takes place, it is extremely important to keep the focus on improving the business processes in need of change, rather than adopting the technology and developing its use. A firm should take a holistic look at its business operations to identify the most significant threats and opportunities. RFID should play a role in completing and enhancing the business processes involved and helping to create a leading system. The best advice is to create self-funding opportunities early that meet the normal return on investment guidelines applied to other investments, but generate short-term paybacks through labor cost reductions, capital avoidance, better asset management, inventory shrinkage, less out-of-stock costs, and customer service improvements. Some firms have found the way to modify their drive for compliance to include some internal improvement features and create better solutions.

Surveys conducted among a sizeable number of industries and companies have identified the following categories of business problems for which the companies believe RFID will help provide solutions:

- Shipping and receiving costs and time
- Inventory management and reductions to shrink and obsolescence
- Data quality across many supply chain links
- Greater visibility into the supply chain network
- Reduced out-of-stocks at the store level and moment of purchase
- Potential to share meaningful data and collaborate with supply chain partners
- Better production control — through more accurate matching of supply with demand
- Reduced theft
- Lower warranty and repair costs

THE ENDGAME BECOMES WIRELESS INVENTORY TRACKING

Thanks to the mandates issued by Wal-Mart, the DOD, and many others, deployment of wireless inventory-tracking systems is moving at a fast pace. At the same time, the field of wireless technology is making great strides, indicative of an emerging trend and the importance of having ubiquitous access to all constituents of a supply chain network. Through wireless technology, suppliers, manufacturers, distributors, retailers, and any necessary third party or intermediary can have untethered access to exactly what is happening within a total system. With the expected removal of constraints to the adoption of wireless technology, such as disparate standards, low bandwidths, and high infrastructure costs, wireless is being adopted for a host of applications — voice and messaging, handheld devices, Internet-enabled equipment, and data networking.

Computers are being connected to allow remote monitoring and data acquisition, to provide access control and security, and to introduce a solution for environments where wires may not be appropriate. Cellular phones, pagers, and two-way business radios can now provide voice and messaging services. Internet-enabled cell phones and personal digital assistants have appeared to connect users to the Internet across a wireless system. New protocols have been introduced just for these devices. Wireless local area networks, for example, can provide the final few feet of access to mobile users and wired systems within a building, restaurant, store, or home.

Broadband wireless is another emerging technology that allows simultaneous delivery of voice, data, and video and could become a competitor to digital subscriber lines. It can enable high-speed connections directly to the key supply chain participants and information they seek, whenever they choose. Ultra-wideband technologies are also being used, to bring the convenience and mobility of wireless communications to high-speed connections in devices appearing throughout the business world.

Bluetooth has come on the scene as a technology specification for low-cost, short-range (up to ten meters) links between mobile PCs, phones, and other handheld devices, with connectivity to the Internet. The Bluetooth wireless technology comprises hardware, software, and interoperability requirements, providing a bridge to existing data networks. Companies promoting this technology include some impressive names: 3Com, Ericsson, IBM, Intel, Lucent, Motorola, and Nokia. Consider a call of importance somewhere in the supply chain that can jump directly to the Internet, bypassing conventional telephone lines and avoiding typical tolls, high costs, and fees. The call can be transferred anywhere in the world, easily covering the extremities of the supply network.

All of these developments, with more to come, are introducing businesses to a world without wires. Today, most communication systems require wires to record, play, or exchange data. The wireless technologies will allow people to dewire their offices and create virtual global systems of connectivity. A supplier that wants to alert a system regarding a pending shortage could put a mobile PC on a desk and instantly connect to a customer's printer, scanner, or Voice over Internet Protocol (VoIP) headset. A mobile computer user who needs to transfer this knowledge could wirelessly connect to a digital projector in a conference room to deliver the message.

Now fit RFID into this scenario. RFID simply connects your assets and inventory to the Internet — wirelessly and at the unique item level. Instead of speculation or interpretation of actual events, you gain real-time visibility into location and condition. More importantly, you gain the ability to act on real-time information. Imagine a five-store promotion of a new product introduction. Even with RFID at the case level, you can view product movement and adjust product availability to meet real-time demand. For example, Wal-Mart is posting product movement data through its RFID read points within its supply chain 30 minutes after the read event has occurred. Supply chain execution management software at the supplier can use this information to adjust and manage product to where it is needed most.

THE EXECUTION PLAN ESTABLISHES THE PILOTS AND ROLLOUT

When all of these factors are considered and the strategy is formalized, as a vital link in the greater business strategy and operating plans, the firm is ready to begin implementation. The execution plan that supports this phase should include setting up pilots for testing and verification. This technique will be covered in detail in Chapter 10. However, we advise that these pilots be well defined and relatively quick. Three months is usually more than adequate to test the pilot hypothesis and gain enough information to make adjusts to the deployment plan. To minimize the risk, these pilots could also include simulations of actual conditions, so real values can be determined before putting too much at stake. Acceptance or rejection will depend on documented results. With the accumulation of the test results, acceptance and rejection will be based far less on simple compliance and speculation and more on elements that support the new strategy and guarantee a reasonable return on investment.

CASE ILLUSTRATION

A case study will help illustrate how a firm moves through an analysis of the potential of RFID and first establishes a vision of where it wants to go with applications and then builds a solid model and strategy for execution. Our case firm is Marks & Spencer, a British retailer selling entirely proprietary-branded products, with annual turnover of $15 billion. Its food division sells almost $7 billion of merchandise per year, equating to 150 million cases of annual through-put. Marks & Spencer Foods has 200 suppliers, many of which are fully dedicated to the firm. The company operates six stockless regional distribution centers that service 400 stores, replenishing stores twice per day without having to carry back room inventories. It is a very fast supply chain that operates with 24-hour supplier-order-to-shelf lead time for key categories of product. Many stores receive daily deliveries, with a delivery window of 15 minutes.

The Opportunity

Marks & Spencer Foods utilizes reusable plastic trays to transport a significant percentage of merchandise through its supply chain. In 2001, the organization decided to replace the tray pool, moving from an imperial to a metric footprint. A compelling business case existed, based on improved vehicle and warehouse utilization. This program necessitated the removal and replacement of all trays and presented Marks & Spencer with a unique opportunity to embrace RFID technology. The decision was taken to "tag" all trays prior to their release into the network at a cost of $0.75 per tray.

Marks & Spencer developed a pragmatic business case for an RFID-enabled food supply chain. The model was based upon a reduction in operating costs and an improvement in business process execution. It is worth noting that RFID potentially provides a significantly greater opportunity in the form of reduced waste, increased availability, and thus, improved sales. However, while there is little doubt such benefits will be enjoyed, these metrics are notoriously difficult to isolate and attribute to a single factor, thus endangering the robustness of the business case.

The Early Stages

The company performed extensive testing of the robustness and applicability of RFID technology under live conditions, focusing on the impact of environmental conditions and operator behavior on read accuracy and speed. With a "clean bill of health," the program moved through to pilot stage, where RFID could be applied within an operational environment. This process enabled Marks & Spencer to evolve the hardware, software, and business processes to maximize potential benefits. For example, the tag readers installed at retail distribution centers (RDCs) evolved through four iterations before a truly ergonomic design was successfully developed. Once a deployable solution had been signed off on, the supply base was engaged and rollout commenced in earnest.

The Solution

Prior to RFID implementation, Marks & Spencer Foods used single-trip bar-coded labels to capture and communicate tray-level information. However, due to the fast-moving nature of the operation and the need for tray-level scanning, the only point at which stock could be scanned was at RDC receipt. This condition caused conflict with suppliers over order accuracy. Similarly, no auditable control existed to ensure pick and dispatch accuracy from RDC to store. Consequently, future supplier orders and store replenishments were derived from inaccurate system stock positions, thus impacting availability and waste.

The RFID strategy, as illustrated in Figure 4.5, involved equipping all supplier premises and Marks & Spencer RDCs with RFID readers/writers. The speed with which RFID technology transmits data ensured that suppliers could write product data to the tag at the point of production (overwriting any previous data) and generate an accurate dispatch manifest without adversely impacting delivery timeliness. RDCs could likewise capture dispatch details for store deliveries, ensuring store stock file integrity. The tray-level bar code scan on RDC intake was naturally replaced by an RFID bulk data capture, which generated significant savings in direct labor costs.

The high-level process clearly illustrates a robust commercial handoff between supplier and retailer, improving collaborative working practices. Although the solution requires suppliers to invest capital in RFID reading/writing technology, Marks & Spencer can point to numerous examples where suppliers have seized the opportunity and, through improved efficiency and reduced punitive charges, realized payback on investment in less than six months.

The schematic also illustrates the positive impact of RFID on stock replenishment. By crediting the store stock file with accurate delivery data, a foundation is created for replenishment systems to generate accurate supplier orders and effectively allocate stock to stores. Such a process prevents the cycle of deterioration created by basing decisions on increasingly inaccurate stock positions.

Conclusion

Unlike many early adopters of RFID in a supply chain environment, Marks & Spencer has progressed well beyond the pilot phase. The metrication program and closed-loop supply chain have been key enablers of the rapid success of the project. Marks & Spencer can today directly attribute significant bottom-line savings to its RFID implementation and has fully justified its original business case for investment in an RFID-enabled supply chain.

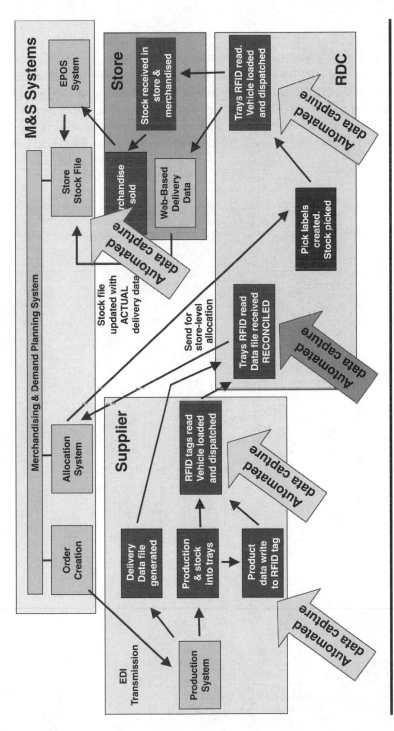

Figure 4.5. Case Study: Marks & Spencer Foods RFID-Enabled Supply Chain Vision

SUMMARY

Promises and problems are included in the continuing debate surrounding acceptance or denial of the RFID technology. Our analysis favors the advocates in this situation, and we have outlined a methodology for developing an RFID strategy, as an adjunct to an existing strategy and business plan. Analyzing all of the factors involved and the potential impact on the key stakeholders will help determine whether the path forward should include acceptance or rejection of RFID.

5

RFID IN SECURITY APPLICATIONS

With at least a framework in place for developing an RFID strategy to complement the business strategy and operating plan, a firm turns its attention next to what technology applications are best suited for its particular business environment. This move requires a company to carefully review what is happening in its marketplace and in business in general, to complete the strategy with an eye for making certain its particular needs have been met. Over the next several chapters, we will pay attention to this merging of RFID applications with the business plan as we explain the future course of RFID deployment as an enabler to supply chain visibility and wireless technology.

Special attention will be given to securing a business from two aspects that tend to receive less attention in supply chain improvement efforts: defeating those who would invade a business for the purposes of bringing harm and those who want to illegally copy a branded product and sell it in a gray market. Intrusion into a supply chain for nefarious purposes and producing fake copies of what is produced have become major concerns to a modern business.

SECURITY HAS BECOME A BIG SUPPLY CHAIN ISSUE

There are many areas in which RFID is being considered a catalyst for improvement. Indeed, the business world is littered with stories of all type in a myriad of industries covering a variety of subjects, many of which have already been mentioned. With the events of 9/11 as one driving factor, consideration of RFID applications has moved to the forefront of attention for security purposes. From another aspect, fake goods have become so common that they represent a serious threat to almost any industry and business. Combating these dual concerns is the subject of this chapter, as we explore the technology being developed to provide safer conditions within supply chain processing.

It matters little whether a company needs to secure people, places, packages, parcels, or products. Some form of individual identification, controlled access to that information, and accurate tracking of movement are the essential elements for guaranteeing security in a supply chain. With the now familiar temporary visitor badges at secured business sites and the employee ID cards used for access to biometric efforts to help prevent the spread of disease, RFID continues its inexorable move toward acceptance. The ability to track, secure, and authenticate assets is just another step on that path toward what could be totally secured environments.

As we begin to elaborate on the appearance of RFID as a security measure, be prepared for some unusual possibilities. Jenny Craig, Inc., for example, realized that security for its 515 nationwide weight-control centers was being managed remotely, resulting in excessive cost for maintenance and a lack of visibility into what was happening across its full supply chain. As a result, the firm developed a strategy to simplify its security management and save some money. The resultant implementation was harmonized with plans for a new data warehouse and web-based client profiling application that would be full of sensitive customer data. Safeguards would play a dual role: providing the needed security of information and reducing costs.

Fortinet, Inc. was selected to provide elements for the network security system overhaul, which moved Jenny Craig from a reliance on old software loaded onto each personal computer that remotely dialed into the corporate offices. The company had been accustomed to routing all of its web traffic from its retail centers through a dedicated server at headquarters, which created a serious information bottleneck. That bottleneck has been removed and Jenny Craig's antivirus and security rule updates are now automatic, enabling the company to spot a security incident immediately. "Before, we didn't see things. Now we can look in one place and see what's happening in each of the centers," says Jeff Nelson, IT director (Hulme 2005a).

THE SECURITY VISION STARTS THE QUEST FOR SPECIFIC IMPROVEMENT

Protection of people, products, and packages is, of course, a never-ending challenge. The threats of counterfeiting, pure mistakes, and terrorist activities have become another part of our everyday living. Just how big is the problem?

Consider the area of counterfeiting, once the bane of federal agents trying to track down the printing presses producing fake dollar bills. Counterfeiting has blossomed into a multibillion-dollar industry, and the list of products affected would fill a book. Aside from the traditional knockoffs of Louis Vitton purses, Gucci clothing, and Rolex watches, the products cover the spectrum of goods. Pfizer's Lipitor and Viagra; Hewlett-Packard ink-jet cartridges; Unilever soaps, shampoos, and tea; Disney videos; AC Delco brake pads; and Buick, Chrysler, and Mitsubishi windshields appear on the new list.

Using state-of the-art equipment to duplicate the originals, Callaway golf clubs, Kyocera cell phone batteries, Yamaha motorcycles, and Gillette's Duracell batteries are on another hot list. Shanghai customs officials inspecting a shipment of motorcycles bound for Dubai peeled off stickers on the bikes that read Honling, only to find Yamaha underneath (Balfour 2005, p. 60). Brewer Anheuser-Busch found serious counterfeiting of its product in China, where locals were retrieving used bottles and filling them with their version of Budweiser.

But techniques to combat the problems are escalating as well. It becomes a dynamic game, as the forces intent on defrauding or beating a system work hard to find and exploit any vulnerabilities no matter how effective a deterrent system might be. In one effort to protect brands and distribution channels, for example, companies are turning to their labeling and tracking systems to protect their products. Figure 5.1 is repeated from Chapter 2 as a generalized depiction of the vision behind the fight-back effort. It points out areas where RFID can be applied to make supply chains more secure. Pfizer, for example, is planning to use RFID tags on Viagra to ensure the right product is being consumed. In China, Anheuser-Bush has introduced temperature-sensitive labels on its bottle that turn red when cold, stumping the counterfeiters for a while.

From whatever source, foreign supplier or local manufacturer, the shipments need to have clear identification of what is contained inside. As the package proceeds to a holding area or distribution center, some form of electronic product code information must be easily accessed to determine product and content data — the more, the better. Anywhere in transit, there should be a means of alerting viewers to the presence of any nonvalid entries. As the journey progresses to the store or consumer — to the back room or from a display rack — the system must be able to continue to track the container and its contents, including recording the quantities being withdrawn or consumed. The Electronic Product Code (EPC) data listed should be considered the opening ante in this situation, as usage and longer journeys are sure to increase the amount of information being accessed.

RFID will eventually play a central role in this picture, as any step across this processing becomes an area where security can be breached, and it is to

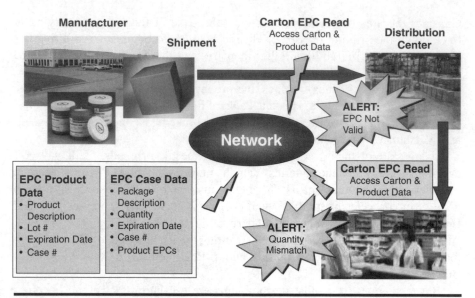

Figure 5.1. Potential Vision to Secure Supply Chain

prevent such situations that the supply chain security measures are being constructed. Developing a security plank for the RFID strategy, however, requires specific areas or problems that have a high need for resolution — pharmaceuticals and medicines, branded products, aerospace and automotive parts, telecommunication equipment, foods and canned goods, and so forth.

Product counterfeiting causes enormous economic damage to firms trying to prevent the unauthorized copying or duplication of their products. Table 5.1 describes the dollar value of counterfeit and pirate product seizures by U.S. Customs and Border Protection. These data represent, of course, only the goods that were seized. The World Customs Organization estimates that "counterfeiting accounts for 5 to 7% of global merchandise trade, equivalent to a loss of as much as $512 billion" in 2004 (Balfour 2005, p. 56). An average company involved in the transfer of intellectual property can spend $2 to $4 million a year on product protection security, but counterfeit goods continue to flood the market, accounting for 8 percent of all world trade, according to the International Chamber of Commerce (Zebra Technologies 2003, p. 2). Bear in mind that reliable estimates peg the amount of counterfeit videotapes coming from China at 95 percent.

The leading protective measures against such activity are constant vigilance and product authentication — using special markings to verify authenticity. The intelligent authenticity offered by RFID, and its ability to read variable information and compare it against what should be represented by the correct ID,

Table 5.1. Counterfeit and Pirate Product Seizures

Year	Value of Seizure	Percent Change
2000	$45 million	—
2001	$57 million	27
2002	$98 million	72

Source: U.S. Customs and Border Protection and International Anti-Counterfeiting Coalition

acts like a constraint within this scenario. Secure media becomes part of this measure as a cost-effective means to protect goods from illegal copying or transfer throughout a supply chain network, including any reverse logistics. Secure media can be used with printers, for example, to create labels for pallets or cartons, which can be applied at any point in distribution, including by wholesalers, distributors, and transportation providers.

The ideal solution makes it extremely difficult for counterfeiters to copy a product code. It also serves to detect such attempts anywhere in the supply chain and to act as a deterrent to would-be thieves. This ideal is achieved by combining, or what is called layering, several types of protection that offer different levels of security. Carefully chosen adhesives can provide tamper-resistant and tamper-evident layers to the tag. Preprinted logos, special artwork, and overvarnishes can incorporate even more security features, while giving the product a consumer-friendly appearance. The printer then adds variable information by encoding the RFID chip within the media. Zebra Technologies makes a line of printers to support such secure media applications.

A variety of invisible taggants are also available to help beef up security. These are engineered materials that can be very accurately verified. They have specific optic or chemical qualities that make them invisible to the naked eye, providing another covert layer of security that is difficult for counterfeiters to detect or reproduce. These taggants resist heat and can be read through overcoatings and other materials applied during the label-making process. Information can often be printed on top of the taggant as well. Adding particularly aggressive adhesives allows a label to self-destruct if it is removed after application, leaving behind a visible mark of the removal, so stolen labels cannot be reused.

Secure media not only offers a security advantage; it can be used for almost any type of product or packaging, from branded goods to industrial parts, leading to further supply chain efficiencies. A few examples illustrate that point:

■   Authentication of critical and expensive supplies or subassemblies to a manufacturing operation, especially proprietary subassemblies that contain unique and innovative materials

- Product verification from the source to use with labels that can be read, data captured from production, work-in-process tracked automatically, and interfaces created with control systems to follow the flow of finished goods
- Variable information like test data, batch codes, operator's information, and key dates added and stored in the tag
- Protection against unauthorized diversion of shipments and missing items in forward shipping
- Creation of accurate bills of lading for authentication by the receiver, eliminating forged documents used to disguise the loss of materials in transit
- Assistance with the inspection and auditing of distribution centers to verify contents and inventories, enabling fast detection of fake goods moving through legitimate channels

Return fraud is another specific problem, for example, which costs U.S. retailers $2 billion annually, according to the National Retail Association. False warranty claims are another major issue plaguing manufacturers, as well as improper maintenance, which leads to premature failures of equipment. In this latter case, one test equipment manufacturer attacked the problem by using smart labels to prevent expired or unauthorized supplies from being used in its machines. "A smart label on each supply cartridge encodes the product type and expiration date. When cartridges are loaded, an RFID reader built into the machine authenticates the cartridge, checks the expiration date and performs calibration specific to the type of cartridge being used" (Zebra Technologies 2003, p. 6).

Medical equipment manufacturers are also testing the combination of using intelligent machines equipped with RFID readers that are capable of interrogating various subassemblies or attachments to ensure that the correct device is being used.

SEPTEMBER 11, 2001 HAD A MAJOR IMPACT ON SECURITY

From one particular aspect, the events of 9/11 ushered in a specific set of conditions that have forever changed the way business will be conducted in the United States and abroad. There may have been a time when companies moved materials on a global basis without too much concern for control. Containers moving from ports to ship were inspected about 15 percent of the time. That was during the time when the government believed that it was in full control of inbound and outbound product movements. During this time, the U.S. Customs Service thought it could focus the majority of its efforts on revenue collection through duties, harbor maintenance fees, and merchandise processing fees.

September 11 became the bell ringer that drove the U.S. government to reevaluate its priorities with regard to the areas being targeted for enforcement. Customs also recognized that there was no way its traditional department activities could attack and control threats of terrorism. Support would need to come from a number of supply chain participants. This shift in national thinking has forced supply chains to restructure global procurement, for example, to assure the security of the purchased products until received into visible inventory. This emphasis on in-transit security also creates a delicate balancing act between commerce and security. Security measures that are too costly or cumbersome will not be rapidly adopted, and delays in shipments can be extremely expensive for the globally sourced organization. However, the reality since 9/11 is that security is now a vital component of any supply chain.

From still another aspect, 9/11 introduced the public to the unpalatable truth that the United States is not invincible. One result of that understanding was the creation of the Department of Homeland Security (DHS). In an effort to improve national security, the U.S. Customs Service was combined with the Immigration and Naturalization Service to form Customs and Border Protection, which was placed under the direction of DHS. This move was intended to show one face at the border, with people and cargo screened by a unified body. Because staffing became a problem, the DHS introduced the Customs-Trade Partnership Against Terrorism (C-TPAT). The purpose of C-TPAT was to challenge both Customs and the trade community to design a new approach to supply chain security, while continuing to allow legitimate business to flow through U.S. borders. In the process, Customs has laid the foundation for the development of a Supply Chain Security Profile, which outlines criteria for a company to compare itself and to measure the similarities and differences.

The C-TPAT program consists of a four-step process:

- Potential participants sign a memorandum of understanding stating that they agree to comply with the program's security guidelines.
- The companies involved then sign a document detailing their current security practices and those of their transportation service providers and overseas suppliers.
- Customs and Border Protection reviews the document and either provisionally accepts the application or asks for an improved security plan.
- Customs and Border Protection inspectors make site visits to verify the information in the application.

Currently, participation in C-TPAT is voluntary, but it is fast becoming a business condition required by such large importers as Home Depot, JC Penney, and Target. The emphasis is initially being placed on foreign suppliers and manufacturers, but the movement can be expected to be extended globally to include ocean carriers, freight forwarders, customs brokers, and port authorities. In view of the burgeoning number of firms that will eventually be involved, if Customs is to deliver on its promise to process goods across borders faster and with less inspection, a tool like RFID must play a role in the identification and tracking processes. Expected benefits include greater visibility into end-to-end movements, automating processes to improve shelf availability for products in greatest demand, and reduced shipping, receiving, and clearance turnaround time.

In January 2005, the U.S. federal government began testing RFID technology at key ports of entry as part of the move to improve its border management system. Visitors entering the country are issued RFID tags which contain serial codes that link to securely stored visitors' information, which will be used to track movements at border crossings. The tamper-proof tags do not include personal or biometric information and will contain a feature to prevent skimming or the use of unauthorized reading devices to capture information from RFID tags.

Border crossings in Arizona, New York, and Washington are on the docket for the period from July 2005 through the spring of 2006. Customs is using RFID in a variety of ways to combat problems, ranging from electronic manifests required 24 hours before a ship leaves a port to viewing videos of what is being loaded and checking the contents inside a container. "Through the use of radio-frequency technology, we see the potential to not only improve the security of our country," says Asa Hutchinson, DHS undersecretary for border and transportation security, "but also make the most important infrastructure enhancements to the U.S. land borders in more than 50 years. We intend to see that it's done in the right way and at the right place." Typical of the two sides in the argument, Jay Stanley, spokesman for the American Civil Liberties Union, expressed concern that "the technology will infringe on privacy rights. It permits automatic, invisible ID checks by the government" (Chabrow 2005a).

The results can be very rewarding for a carefully deployed application. According to Toby Gooley, managing editor of *Logistics Management,* "C-TPAT program managers say that members' shipments are inspected three to five times less often than imports in general, and they are subject to enforcement actions six to eight times less often." According to Gooley, "[Toy maker] Hasbro has been able to process more than 99 percent of its entries entirely without paper. It has also reduced the number of Customs holds from 211 out of nearly 2800 entries in 2001 to 45 out of 4100 in 2003, and the number of intensive physical inspections has plummeted from 31 in 2001 to just 5 last year" (Gooley 2005, p. 12). Gooley notes that other importers have found unexpected opportunities for improving efficiency because C-TPAT requires them to document procedures and inspect overseas plants.

Another example of the use of RFID to secure our borders can be seen by Customs and Border Protection's implementation of FAST (Free and Secure Trade) at selected border crossings between at the U.S. and Canadian and U.S. and Mexican borders. This voluntary program allows known low-risk participants expedited border processing. Through the combination of precertification of importers in each country, RFID windshield decals, risk management principles, and supply chain security, this program allows Customs officials to focus their efforts on higher risk shipments.

An illustration of how technologies are being merged to create a totally secure environment comes from the DHS, which began required fingerprinting and photographing of visa holders entering the United States by year-end 2003. Visitors who require a visa will have each index finger scanned, with digitized information linked via a private DHS network to an undisclosed repository for cross-checking with existing prints of terrorists or criminals. Border agents will also digitally photograph visitors and check the entry photo against the picture founding the visa. A screening process upon departure was implemented as well, beginning in 2004 (Chabrow 2003).

In yet another effort to secure the United States, Customs has also developed a program specifically designed to protect against future terrorist attacks. Called the Container Security Initiative, this program was designed to push U.S. borders further out. In the process, Customs identified 25 major seaports that account for almost 89 percent of all container traffic into the United States and has deployed Customs officers to those ports. Once there, these officials work with their host nation counterparts to target high-risk cargo containers. Within the DHS, Customs' main principle is that the United States will be the last line of defense, rather than the first point of attack.

CONTAINER CONTENTS AND IDENTIFICATION BECOME CRITICAL

From the view of identifying what can be contained in shipments to the United States, Customs has been using available and planned technologies. Bar coding has the current dominant role, but RFID is rapidly taking center stage to keep track of what is crossing borders, coming in and going out. In cooperation with the retailer's Secure Supply Chain Initiative, the manufacturer attaches an RFID tag to its shipping containers, trays, and pallets, at its national distribution center, before any loading and shipment to retail store warehouses. From the manufacturer's perspective, RFID becomes a tool for meeting compliance with the U.S. security mandates and a means to track shipments all the way to the retailer's store shelves.

The traditional black-line bar codes have been around the retail world for decades. RFID tags now provide the ability to program a smart tag with multiple pieces of information, not just an identification number. With its programmable chip and readers at strategic locations, RFID affords the opportunity to track shipments from end to end in the global supply chain — to not only provide trace-and-trace information but to provide active alerts on product environment (humidity, shock, temperature, presence of radiation, etc.) at the unique item level. Armed with this information, the process becomes one of proactive supply change management versus reactive problem or situation resolution. There is no longer a need for manual keying and manipulation of handheld bar scanners. Inventory is tracked before loading for export, as the pallets are driven past readers in any storage area, and forward to and backward from the stores, to capture any stock being returned.

RFID opens new doors for automated inventory control, transactions in global procurement, and greater security in the supply chain processes related to global commerce. A bar code label, for example, cannot be placed on the side of a shipping vessel. It might be placed on the side of a shipping container, but an RFID tag can be placed on every item within all of the containers going on a particular ship. RFID readers can scan many items at once, while bar coding is limited to one-at-a-time scanning. Consider the greater ease of a mixed pallet of product or containers within containers moving through a busy port, not having to be touched and having a single read identify all contents. As an aid to Customs, allowing that organization to identify what is in any load, another RFID application is started in the areas of clearance and security.

Global standards will be a crucial element in any successful transition, but through the efforts of EPCglobal and other bodies, the international community is cooperating to overcome this hurdle. Any standard will be used with the unique identification (UID) endorsed by the U.S. Department of Defense, as that organization has deemed UID as established and to be used to control its annual $80 billion of transactions.

SECURING A SUPPLY CHAIN

With heightened attention to security on an international basis, businesses are now forced to consider how to make a supply chain less vulnerable and as secure as possible. How to accomplish such an arduous task is foremost in a

Figure 5.2. Metro AG RFID Will Be Integral to Store Operations

supply chain manager's mind, along with the need to create greater efficiencies and customer satisfaction. Inspecting every package or container is one approach, but clearly not an economical solution. A better system begins by taking the vision to a few carefully selected suppliers and together working out the possible routes to success. Figure 5.2 illustrates such an effort. Metro AG, the Germany-based retailer referenced earlier, decided that RFID would be an integral part of store operations, to help in the fight against theft and inventory shrinkage. Networked tag readers would be placed strategically throughout the store, including on shopping carts. Tags would be placed inconspicuously on actual items, such as razor blade cartridges, medicines, and high-value SKUs. A control system would monitor daily activities and report any aberrations, such as the removal from the shelf of an unusually high quantity of items, a sure indication of shoplifting.

Selecting the right partner with which to test such a strategy is a critical step in the process and one worthy of serious attention. Rinehart et al. have presented a very good paper on this subject in which they define a framework for evaluating and differentiating suppliers so those most likely to exhibit a strong security ethic can be determined. The authors outline a simple but effective questionnaire and assessment tool to begin such segmentation and define which suppliers rate the most trust and which constitute the greatest risk. They go further to discuss commitments to the relationship and describe seven types of supplier relationships that have unique characteristics, from those where neither party places much trust in the other to those where there is an abundance of interaction and a high level of trust. For each type of relationship, they provide advice on which party should have more or less control over security matters in business activities affecting the relationship (Rinehart et al. 2004).

Across these relationships, a wide variety of smart, sense-and-response devices will increasingly become important links in supply chain technology, according to Thomas Foster, editor of *Global Logistics & Supply Chain Strategies*. Foster points out that Forrester calls these sensors, global positioning system devices, RFID, and other established technologies the "X internet, because sensing data flows from the external device into online planning and execution systems." He explains that "the most publicized X internet examples center on cargo security" (Foster 2004, p. 40).

Concerns surrounding potential terrorist activities using ocean freight and the many containers they carry to smuggle all sorts of unwanted goods have prompted a number of initiatives by DHS, including Smart and Secure Trade Lanes and Operation Safe Commerce, each of which is employing X internet technologies. According to Foster, "One such pilot program includes use of RFID technology placed inside containers to track movement and to sense any attempts to tamper with the contents. Both Hewlett-Packard and Target Stores are participating."

Security issues extend well beyond the ports of entry, of course, and many applications are already well established, such as the familiar passive tags attached to retail goods that send a screeching signal if they remain on an article and pass through a reader at a store door. A form of active tags has also been in use for greater asset protection and access control, such as those placed by Gillette in packages of razor replacement blades. These and other actions are intended to reduce theft, reduce inventory needs, and eventually improve customer satisfaction and increase sales revenues. There is a special need in the pharmaceutical business. Consumers expect their prescription information to be kept private. Suppliers to the industry also expect their product information which might be exposed at various distribution points to be kept from the hands of competitors.

The future of RFID in supply chains will be shaped by many forces, from business and societal factors to economies of scale and technology advances, once again impacted by those representing the advocates and cynics. Gillette's experiments aimed at reducing theft and inventory shrinkage led to a website (www.boycottgillette.com) intended to raise resistance to in-store scanning and what the site sponsors considered spying techniques. Consumers Against Supermarket Privacy Invasion and Numbering (CASPIAN) also appeared, along with www.epic.org/privacy/rfid. Metro was forced, in the face of unfavorable publicity, to end use of radio tags in its frequent-shopper cards.

To take a stab at what will happen in general terms, there are certain expectations that should play into the formation of what does emerge in the area of supply chain security:

- The privacy advocates will win some short-term victories, but not impede RFID moving into commercial supply chains. In spite of concerns raised over activities by Gillette and Metro, there is too much to be gained by these types of organizations to cause them to do more than approach the situation more carefully and to work on appeasing the most vociferous groups, through consumer education and aggressive privacy policies.
- The magical five-cent threshold on chip costs will be breached. Until that time, there are other costs that must be assumed (tags, readers, training, testing, software, and middleware), with paybacks to be developed over several years of application.
- Commercial and military supply chains will be driven initially by electronic product codes (EPC) and UID standards.
- Completion of the Class 1 Gen 2 UHF tag will spur significant R&D developments by major chip manufacturers such as Texas Instruments, Philips, and others, further improving performance and lowering costs.
- Readers and antennas will become commodities within another year, opening the door for serious data mining and warehouse software applications. Companies such as Cisco will develop intelligent readers that will act as routers.
- Smaller, lighter, undetectable, invisible tags will appear with floor-to-ceiling readers. The readers will achieve commonality to the point where a stolen item will set off an alarm in any store in a shopping mall, not just the one from which it was taken.
- Better paper trails will become an element of security, as well as personal shopkeeper identification every time an item's tag is disabled. This technology will brush very close to civil rights legislation and require strict accountability.
- RFID technology will merge with biometrics, retina ID, smart cards, video motion analysis, and traditional physical security systems. Active tags will be used to confirm identity and employee information as well as for inventory management, matching tags of people with those of equipment.

SUMMARY

Security has always been an issue with a supply chain and across or within country borders. The events surrounding 9/11 have brought a heightened awareness to the serious effects that can occur from a lax system. The proliferation of counterfeiting has exacerbated the situation, making security a crucial issue to supply chain managers. In this chapter, we have positioned the need for applications that include RFID technology. In future chapters, we will continue the theme, as we look at how specific applications of merit are emerging across a typical supply chain network.

6

RFID IN
THE DEFENSE SECTOR

There is a revolution going on within military groups throughout the world, especially among the United States and its allies, focused on improving what happens in any theater of operation. At the center of the revolution are the intentions to avoid mistakes of the past and to take advantage of best commercial practices, so the military forces in action can be better enabled to dominate an adversary. Crucial to this vision is the need to take what amounts to a network-centric view of warfare, sustained by enhanced supply chain systems that are far superior to those of the enemy, no matter how extended the linkages. This latter requirement demands that the military force, including all important allies, have visibility into its supply chain and can access and deploy goods through a wireless communication environment.

Modern warfare involves global coalitions. Across these extended military enterprises, constrained operations, lack of essential supplies, and missing components must be banished. In their place, there must be agile logistics systems with clear visibility into what is in storage by exact location, what is in transit and in use, and what can be accessed at times of emergency. Like any commercial supply chain network, such a system is only as good as the weakest link, so there must be accurate and efficient collaboration across the end-to-end processing.

This chapter dissects what is behind the mandates by the U.S. Department of Defense (DOD) and the military services to adopt unique identification (UID) and eventually RFID technology in their supply chain, as soon as possible. As we review what is transpiring, keep in mind that the DOD has probably the most complex supply chain in the world. It manages four million SKUs, from 43,000 suppliers — from shoes and socks to parts for armored vehicles, blood plasma, and ammunition. The U.S. Defense Logistics Agency (DLA), which provides materiel to the military services (Army, Navy, Marines, and Air Force), operates 18 large distribution depots in the United States. Add in the facilities operated by the services for maintenance and parts storage and mobile bases around the globe, and the complexity becomes a challenge to optimize.

The chapter also deals with what is transpiring in aerospace, as that industry keeps pace with the military. While the mandated dates have been extended, make no mistake — the defense sector has no intention of backing down from full compliance by all suppliers. U.S. government spending on the technology is predicted by some analysts to rapidly increase 120 percent by 2009 (Jacques 2005). The concept of RFID as a means for enabling electronic labeling and wireless identification of objects using radio frequency communication is too compelling to disregard. What is required is the construction of a systems architecture, already under way, which will handle the expected deluge of information.

BRIEF HISTORICAL VIEW

Organizations connected with the aerospace and defense industries have always tried to work on the front edge of technology to gain an advantage. From early moves into Internet technology and such efforts as replacing heavy metals with stronger composites, introducing guidance and positioning systems, and developing enterprise resource planning, both sectors have been hard at work defining, testing, and implementing better capabilities. Superiority is a driving force here, as being in the forefront of a successful initiative is considered tantamount to having an advantaged position. As a result, expensive initiatives are generally accepted as the price of radically improving operational effectiveness. As the technologies provide proof of value, implementations typically accelerate. Such will be the case with testing and deployment of RFID technology, the latest potential game-winning advancement.

The DOD has been quick to issue its policy mandating future application of the technology, forcing investment in the still-emerging concepts to achieve compliance. Companies that are following the mandates are finding, however, that they can also achieve improvements by leveraging their new systems over other supply chain activities. These benefits include better inventory management, less shrinkage, asset visibility, and improved end-to-end supply chain processing, typically with the same or fewer labor hours. It is becoming less a matter of "I guess we have no choice but to comply" and more " I think there's something in here for all of us."

The DOD policy essentially covers both active and passive tags (with passive tags being the early favorite) and dictates the adoption of specific business rules that will position DOD as an early adopter, with the intention of helping willing suppliers to find ways to recover their costs. According to RFID guidelines released by DOD, "military agencies and branches will include the tagging requirement in contracts for suppliers that ship packaged troop rations, clothing, individual equipment and tools, personal items, and weapon systems repair parts and components to the two DLA facilities" in California and Pennsylvania (Violino 2005, p. 33). Early efforts are already providing the intended results with passive tags. While some of the suppliers approached the transition as moving from bar coding to RFID, the discovery has been that a combination will exist for some time, but RFID will provide special advantages through the ability of the products to literally communicate among themselves. Such activity allows for frequent and effective tracking of materiel, containers, and transport vehicles under conditions of real-time visibility and control.

LESSONS FROM DESERT STORM

In Figure 6.1, we see that the situation in the Gulf War, or Operation Desert Storm, created special logistics problems that helped push the mandates forward. There were no warehouses near the center of action that could be accessed, and open spaces could be anything but friendly. This operation left the

Figure 6.1. Cross-Docking in Desert Storm

U.S. military subject to criticism of its existing logistics practices. On the one hand, the war effort was accomplished quickly in spite of enemy claims of overwhelming advantage and superior numbers. The necessary supplies were accumulated and deployed to the theater of action, supporting U.S. and allied forces, and the battle was settled swiftly.

On the other hand, the U.S. military could not identify the contents of over 28,000 shipping containers, representing almost 60 percent of those deployed in support of military personnel (Macmillan-Davies 2003, p. 8). When the military mission was concluded, the lack of an integrated identification and tracking system meant the organizations needing supplies now sitting in a Middle Eastern desert could not locate what had become surplus items, for reuse on new missions. Some of the inventory subsequently seemed to vanish without a trace.

Faced with the perpetual need to know where its supplies might be, from pallets to cartons and individual items, and in view of the necessity to do a better job with future efforts, the DOD has been hard at work bringing focus to satisfying its ultimate consumer — the battle-ready war fighter. Congress entered this picture with mandates of its own that the DOD should adopt best commercial practices, in spite of a history of having some pretty successful practices that were being copied by commercial organizations. A number of improvement efforts ensued, across all services and their support organizations.

In February 2005, over 1,000 representatives from the military and contracting suppliers came together in Washington, D.C. to attend the third DOD RFID Summit for Industry. Stressing once again its strong commitment to and mandates behind RFID usage for military purposes, DOD representatives indicated that supplier-compliant shipments in four categories of materiel had been started at the Susquehanna, Pennsylvania and San Joacquin, California distribution centers. Throughout the two days of discussion between uniformed and civilian military personnel and members of the contracting community, the emphasis was on overcoming the obstacles and meeting the challenges that continue to lie ahead. What was clear to all attendees was the message: DOD's RFID efforts are being carried out for the military customers — soldiers, sailors, and airmen, what this sector refers to as the battle-ready "war fighter." By January 2006, 32 bases and depots, including the Defense Depot in Norfolk, Virginia and the Air Mobility Command Terminal at Norfolk Naval Air Station, will begin to process RFID tags. By 2007, all suppliers and manufacturers shipping to any DOD location will be required to use the tags (Connolly 2005). By about 2010, all pallets and cases shipped to large depots run by the DLA will need to have passive RFID tags as well.

According to Peter Langworthy, director of the AIT Center for Northrop Grumman, the DOD "wants to provide assurances and visibility to the soldiers that the material is getting to them in a timely manner, allowing them to make the decisions they need to carry out their missions." For this Los Angeles–based defense contractor that works primarily with the U.S. Air Force, the issue revolves around how best to comply while making a return on the effort for the company. "We obviously have supply chain and business processes that we do as well. The question is should we be using RFID in those?" (Purdum 2004). Answering that question with a positive attitude helps create the needed alignment across management and drives the search for the total savings potential. Northrop Grumman IT has been awarded a series of RFID contracts from the U.S. government. In 2004, the Williamsburg, Virginia office received $6 million in contracts to produce RFID kits for the military, according to Langworthy.

In a directed move under the DOD, defense logistics has been combined with global supply chain management systems to form DLGSCMS. The undersecretary of defense for acquisition, technology, and logistics was designated as the defense logistics executive, who in turn designated the commander, U.S. Transportation Command (USTRANSCOM) as the distribution process owner. These changes were intended to tighten the military supply chain and include all activities that provide materiel support to the combatant commanders, who could often be unaware of the status of scheduled deliveries. The marching order was to meet future requirements without disruption.

Among the many tests and trials that have ensued, in an attempt to modernize military logistics, there has come a realization that RFID offers benefits for tracking and avoiding a recurrence of the wastes and loss of a large volume of assets from the first Gulf War. The DLA eventually issued a mandate that all military assets would be tracked with RFID tagging by 2003. This process was to be a part of the department's view to start with UID, as illustrated by a variety of existing techniques in Figure 6.2. The expected benefits were to be greatly reduced dependency on inventories and the agility to rapidly deploy war stocks to theaters of operation and specific missions. The policy has gone through a number of revisions, but the intent remains the same. RFID policy requires suppliers to put passive tags on the lowest possible piece — part, case, or pallet — beginning February 2005.

The DOD has focused its early efforts on high-value goods from its suppliers and is not asking these suppliers to bear the tag costs, expecting rather that the costs of the tags will be factored into future procurement contracts. Suppliers will, of course, need to purchase the readers and make investments in the RFID infrastructure (Violino 2005, p. 32). Cradle-to-grave tracking of assets is expected to lead to more efficient supply chain processing and smarter asset management. Safety stocks will be reduced as visibility is maintained from the time an item enters the system, and shortages will be eliminated.

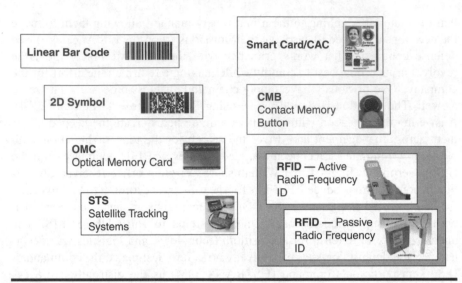

Figure 6.2. DOD Automated Tracking Technologies (Source: www.dodait.com)

Using the inherent technology to provide remote access to data about supplies over a wireless network, RFID will monitor and analyze the location and condition of supplies, machinery, and equipment. The U.S., U.K., and Canadian military supply chains have embraced and begun deploying RFID-based systems.

Conditions improved during Operation Enduring Freedom in Afghanistan, as features of asset visibility and life cycle management began to appear. During that effort, the combatant commander identified the need for "in-the-box visibility" of material entering the combat theater. For military suppliers in the second Gulf War (Operation Iraqi Freedom), the advantages of the technological advances really began to be seen, as the use of active, data-rich RFID tags was mandated for all material entering that theater. The mandate issued in the memo depicted in Figure 6.3 helped drive compliance. The effort moved quickly to attaining conditions of in-transit visibility and ultimately total asset visibility. Using RFID technology, supply staff could now search hundreds of containers and identify the location of specific items, such as a special plasma or size 11 D shoe, without needing to open the container.

Through additional efforts with its logistics modernization effort, the vision is moving toward having the ability to obtain total asset visibility across an entire military inventory, whether in transit, in use, or in process. Logistics personnel, moreover, will be able to monitor the location, condition, and avail-

Ultimately, the warfighter requires visibility in order to exercise directive authority. We must expand active RFID across the log chain, linking the islands to create seamless visibility. At the same time, we must drive RFID as a transactional medium, bringing it into the business and transaction process, rather than continuing to treat it as a parallel universe. We need to develop total asset visibility (TAV), not just in-transit visibility, and include in TAV tactical logistics visibility, extending to the warfighter.

Propent(s)	Office of Primary Responsibility (OPR)
OSD	ADUSD (SCI)

Figure 6.3. Make RFID Real: Operation Iraqi Freedom

ability to plan and execute support for the war fighters. On February 20, 2004, the undersecretary of defense issued an RFID policy update which mandates the use of passive tags at the case, pallet, and UID item packaging level for all solicitations after October 1, 2004 for delivery on or after January 1, 2005. That mandate was extended to February 2005.

RFID IN THE MILITARY ENVIRONMENT

As illustrated in Figure 6.2, we can see the DOD has been using a variety of tracking technologies for some time. Bar codes have a long history, but require visual contact between the scanner and the bar code. RFID, of course, offers the advantage of not needing this line of sight while also providing a much greater level of item detail. Since RFID data are transmitted via radio waves, multiple tags can be read at the same time, from ever-increasing distances. Thousands of tags can be read in a second, regardless of environmental conditions not too foreign to military campaigns — dirt, frost, humidity, and grease. While most bar codes indicate classes of products, they have limited information-carrying capacity and do not possess a unique identifier for each specific item. With RFID, additional information can be added as the item moves toward the theater of need.

While companies in the commercial world continue to search for meaningful applications, the U.S. Navy is already applying RFID to help save lives. Through its Tactical Medical Coordination System (TacMedCS), this service has been simplifying hospital administration, reducing errors, and providing better medical care, under difficult conditions. Each patient admitted into the Navy's Fleet

Hospital Three in Iraq, for example, is tagged with an RFID-enabled wristband that contains unique ID numbers for the duration of treatment. Doctors and nurses scan the bracelet and enter information or diagnoses, treatments, and status, which proceed to a central data system.

TacMedCS replaces the labor-intensive and often flawed manual entry system that dates back to the Civil War. Medics can use the tags on the battlefield to identify the wounded before they are sent to the hospital. Access to the database helps doctors to be better prepared to treat the patient upon arrival. In addition, "Doctors in the United States are able to examine the data carefully to determine if soldiers are suffering common injuries, then try to find ways to prevent that. It also provides a way for researchers to link up to larger health databases and try to understand medical phenomena such as the Gulf War syndrome" (Ewalt 2003, p. 57).

Figure 6.4 illustrates the DOD's call to action, as it spells out the requirements by class code. Palletized unit loads are now required to contain an RFID tag. Any exterior containers must be so equipped as well. UID item unit packs needed a tag by February 2005. All UID packaging required passive tags by

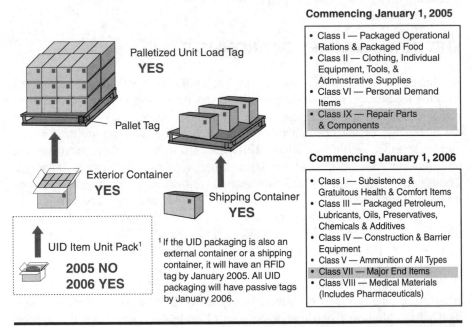

Figure 6.4. DOD RFID Requirements (Source: Office of the Secretary of Defense, RFID Industry Day on July 1, 2004)

A Type 3 temperature and manifest tag is attached to a pallet of rations

Type 1 Electronic Product Code tags are affixed along the edge of individual cases of Meals, Ready-to-Eat

Figure 6.5. DOD RFID Application

January 2006. As an example of how this mandate will be met, in Figure 6.5 we see Electronic Product Code tags affixed to the pallet protection material at the top of loads of meals. In the picture to the right, a Type 3 temperature and manifest tag has been attached to a pallet load of rations.

The UID derivation process is described in Figure 6.6, as the DOD outlined its intention to uniquely identify all materiel in its supply chain. From manufacturing or acquisition and placement of product specifications through delivery to the military and deployment into the theater of action, data will follow the product flow. All unique identifiers will be embedded in the tags, so tracking can be done accurately and on a timely basis, and nothing will be lost. To enable such a system, a variety of automatic identification technology (AIT) devices come into play. Figure 6.7 illustrates some of these devices, including the familiar bar code, an RFID tag, contact memory buttons, optical memory card, and a sample smart card.

The expected advantages cover a wide range of objectives. The military expects to eventually achieve inside-the-box visibility, with all container contents accessed. In-transit visibility will continue, from point of origin through nodes, terminals, depots, and on to final destination. Serial numbers will be tracked throughout the processing, providing access to weapons, high-priority battle needs, and especially sensitive items. Receipt, issue, storage, packing, loading, unloading, and inventorying will be documented and kept live in the system. Unit movement, personnel tracking, and equipment and supplies need

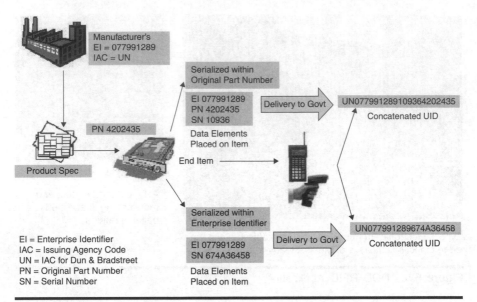

Figure 6.6. UID Derivation Process (Source: DOD Guide to Uniquely Identifying Items, Version 1.3, November 25, 2003)

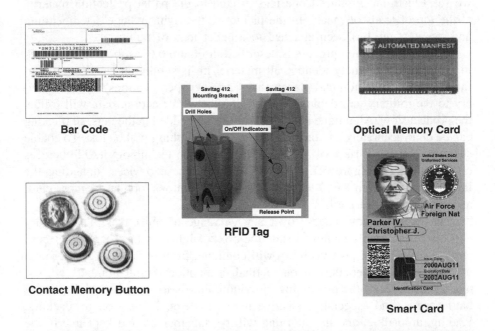

Figure 6.7. AIT Devices

will be within this system. Equipment status reporting and maintenance updates will be available, as well as motor pool dispatching, quality control surveillance, and electronic medical records and patient tracking.

VISIBILITY AND COLLABORATION BECOME HALLMARKS OF SUCCESS

The Honorable Michael S. Wynne, undersecretary of defense, explained why RFID has become so important to the DOD in a speech titled "The Case for Transatlantic Cooperation: A U.S. Perspective." Wynne stated:

> The world's largest retailer, Wal-Mart, figured out before we did that, given the scope of our logistics challenge, we need to go the route of RFID — and quickly. Therefore, we are partnering with Wal-Mart for RFID. Between the two organizations, we will be covering a wide dispersion of manufacturing and distribution. This will effectively open the RFID market by introducing volumes not expected for years in the future. This is a partnering opportunity for all of you as well: We'll be looking for your ideas and innovations in UID and RFID technology. Your support to internationalize these approaches will also be of great help.

Through this explanation and call for collaboration, he set out the view for future military operations, in which the global information grid will spread over the extended military supply chain. From research and development, testing and evaluation, through acquisition, storage, inter- and intratheater movement, and finally to tactical movement and distribution, the joint war fighter requirements will be met with state-of-the-art communications and tracking. Through collaborative efforts across this expansive arena, allies to the military effort will be required to adopt RFID technology and use the devices illustrated to make certain there are no weak or missing links in the system.

When fully functional, conditions as described in Figure 6.8 will prevail, and the combatant commander will be supported with total asset visibility, a central objective of the new military standards. With this visibility, operations can improve its decision making of contingency planning, force allocation, mission assignments, and force readiness. Logisticians will have a better understanding of operational support issues, improving the efficient cross-leveling of supplies by diverting materials to areas of greatest need. The weapons manager can have a better feel for readiness, set priorities for supply, and

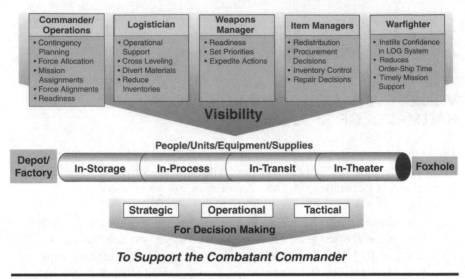

Figure 6.8. Total Military Asset Visibility

expedite correct actions. Item managers will be able to do a better job of redistribution and make better procurement, inventory control, and repair decisions. Finally, the war fighters will have a greater sense of confidence in the logistics system supporting them. They will be able to count on a reduced order-to-ship cycle time and timelier mission support in general. From factory or depot to the foxhole, people, units, equipment, and supplies will be accurately deployed and tracked.

A critical component of this future-state vision will be in-transit visibility (ITV). ITV becomes the capability that uses RFID and AIT to provide the logistics customer with maximum visibility and real-time status on the movement of all classes of supply. It identifies, locates, and tracks the movement of all classes of supply from source of supply to consumption by the end user. The ITV architecture for the military is illustrated in Figure 6.9, where the tags, servers, interrogators, and intermediate components are positioned. Using a combination of cable connections, radio frequency data exchange, and modems for operation, the system will provide the type of in-transit tracking necessary to make total asset visibility work.

Using tag-writing software, data are written to an RFID tag, through either a handheld interrogator or a portal station. The data placed on the RFID tag are obtained from automated information systems, including TC-AIMS II, TC_ACCIS, SARSS, and SAAS-MOD, which are normally loaded on the same computer as the tag-writing software. Tag-writing software also uploads a du-

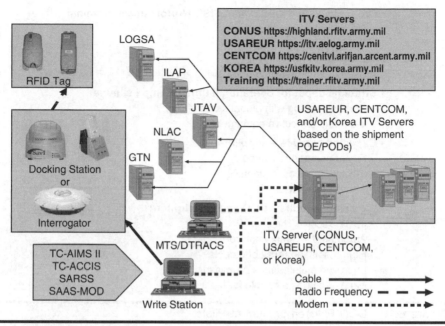

Figure 6.9. ITV Architecture

plicate of the tag data to the regional ITV servers. This step allows tracking of equipment and supplies by doing queries and reports on a regional ITV server. In Figure 6.9, the data sent to a local server will be replicated to other regional ITV servers, based on the point of entry (POE) and point of delivery (POD) of the cargo and equipment being shipped. The CONUS server will receive data on all tags written. The shipment data will be pushed or pulled from the CONUS ITV server to GTN, LOGSA, NLAC, ILAP, and JTAV. As the tagged vehicle, pallet, or container passes interrogators, the location, date, and time group of the shipment is posted on the regional server. For more information on writing to RFID tags, see the AIT/RFID Operations Guide at www.cascom.army.mil/ Automation/ITV/guidebooks/index.htm, developed and hosted by Computer Sciences Corporation.

The present RFID architecture does have one void, which occurs when the cargo leaves the POE and arrives at the POD. For air cargo, this condition is being solved by GATES send tags and event information to the ITV server. The only current solution for sea ports is the use of EEDSK, but the solution should be that warehouse systems would feed the ITV server. Future experiments and pilots will serve to help resolve this and other roadblocks. Figure 6.10 lists two of these anticipated pilots and the expected benefits.

- **Cross-docking operations at FISC Norfolk ocean terminal**
  - Track small shipments
  - Expand to all shipments
  - Eliminate hand scanning
  - Use tag as transaction of record
- **Strategic depot for operational unit – Camp LeJeune**
  - Combat feeding with global asset visibility
  - Individual protective equipment
- **Expected benefits – suppliers**
  - Faster demand response
  - Efficient production planning
  - Recall of defects
- **Expected benefits – DOD and war fighters**
  - Faster receive and ship
  - Automated inventory control
  - High-resolution recall of defects
  - Improved maintenance processes
  - More airplanes available for flight

Figure 6.10. DOD Planned or Current Pilots

PLANNED AEROSPACE ACTIVITIES

In an associated set of activities, the aerospace industry is also moving forward with RFID adoption. In fact, testing of RFID in the industry is moving at a feverish pace, according to Tony Kontzer of *Information Week,* as "carriers and manufacturers try to spot any potential problems in using the technology to improve everything from the parts supply chain to baggage storage handling." Covering the Global Aviation RFID Forum in Atlanta in June 2004, Kontzer reported that FedEx and Delta were planning to begin RFID pilot tests, while Boeing and Airbus S.A.S. were jointly issuing instructions on the use of passive 13.56-MHz tags on aircraft and engine parts. "FedEx and Boeing completed a 90-day joint test in which 40 parts on a FedEx plane — parts ranging from wheel wells to hydraulic pumps to smoke detectors — were tagged with passive chips and transmitters and then read at the conclusion of the flights." No tag deterioration was detected and data collection was rated as 100 percent (Kontzer 2004).

Using standard formats, like that described in Figure 6.11, companies across the industry are progressing with their version of deployment. Boeing and Airbus, for example, have reached agreement on a collaborative approach for adopting uniform standards, as each firm sees large benefits, especially in the tracking and deployment of parts. The two firms held a series of industry forums

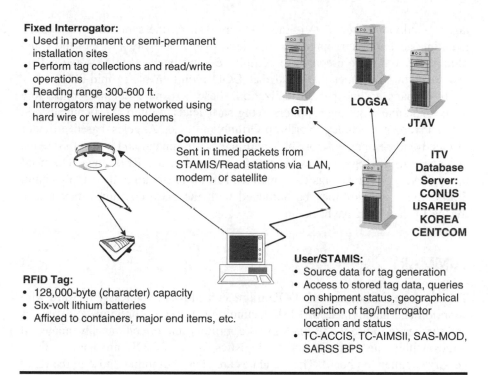

Fixed Interrogator:
- Used in permanent or semi-permanent installation sites
- Perform tag collections and read/write operations
- Reading range 300-600 ft.
- Interrogators may be networked using hard wire or wireless modems

GTN   **LOGSA**   **JTAV**

Communication:
Sent in timed packets from STAMIS/Read stations via LAN, modem, or satellite

ITV Database Server: CONUS USAREUR KOREA CENTCOM

RFID Tag:
- 128,000-byte (character) capacity
- Six-volt lithium batteries
- Affixed to containers, major end items, etc.

User/STAMIS:
- Source data for tag generation
- Access to stored tag data, queries on shipment status, geographical depiction of tag/interrogator location and status
- TC-ACCIS, TC-AIMSII, SAS-MOD, SARSS BPS

Figure 6.11.   RFID Architecture

in Atlanta (June 8, 2005), Hong Kong (August 10, 2005), and Munich (October 19, 2005). A special concern for this group is how to eliminate the entry of unapproved or counterfeit parts into their supply chains.

Of particular interest is the fact that the two companies are determined not to approach the issue in the mandated manner, preferring instead to use a cooperative approach to get the job done. Boeing is not interested in issuing mandates. Instead, it is planning to issue a set of specifications for suppliers. The specifications will detail Boeing's technical standards around such issues as the frequency, memory capacity, and size of the RFID tags and labels. Suppliers shipping to the company will need to label their components with RFID tags that meet these specifications.

From the military perspective, Lockheed Martin, the world's largest defense contractor, has rolled out a phased approach to its passive RFID implementation, spread over several years. Lockheed does not ship to the two DLA depots, so meeting the mandates comes later in the time frame for this industrial giant. The firm is in the process of developing a corporate policy "for tagging all cases and pallets to be shipped to the DOD that carry repairables, electronic components and other equipment. The company is also exploring the possibility of tagging individual items" (Violino 2005, p. 34). At the same time, Lockheed is taking steps to assure its major suppliers (over 2,000) are aware of the DOD requirements and are prepared to comply. Boeing began tagging some pallets and cases in November 2004 and met DOD requirements in mid-2005.

In perhaps an unexpected realization, these aerospace defense contractors have found that requiring suppliers to tag parts leads to internal efficiencies and better inventory accuracy. Northrop Grumman, a Los Angeles–based provider of electronic components for ships and planes, command and control systems, and space technology, is now requiring suppliers to use RFID tags. The need is for these types of savings to be realized further upstream in the supply chain. Some small suppliers may be burdened with the extra cost until they find a means of gaining a payback.

SUMMARY

There can be no stopping the DOD train, as it moves relentlessly forward with adoption and deployment of RFID technology. Based on previous experiences and the desire to use the technology as a military and operations advantage, all forces within the military and the logistics arms of DOD are hard at work getting suppliers on board. The mandates are clear, but unlike those in the retail sector, serious attention is being given to helping the suppliers find a return on the investment. As the effort spreads beyond the February 2005 target date, we expect to see the number of suppliers escalate and the success stories — proving the existence of other values — to drive further acceptance. Aerospace and defense can be counted on to be at the forefront of the pathfinders, especially in light of the high-value mission-critical nature of the components that are shipped, showing the way forward with the RFID technology. With a slew of applications already under way, look for continued emphasis and acceptance across both industries.

7

RFID IN THE RETAIL SECTOR: WHERE GOES THE COST?

From cans of coffee and packs of razor blades to a single pair of shoes, boxes of ammunition, or blood plasma, the supply chain of the future will include stowaway passengers — tiny chips, sometimes the size of a speck of pepper, emitting identifying data to a sensor. What does this mean for a retailer? The answer to this question for a very important supply chain sector revolves around issues less publicized than the expected improvements to information, inventory control, and having the right products on the shelves so there is less chance of out-of-stocks. Labor savings and reduction of internal theft are high on the real list driving deployment. As we review the potential benefits to retailers from the adoption of RFID technology, we will see that labor and theft dwarf the other advantages, providing a typical retailer with the opportunity to more than double profits — or possibly return part of the savings to consumers in the form of lower prices.

At a time when great opportunities are appearing to reap this kind of windfall, the retail sector is faced with the greatest area of pushback from upstream suppliers. The companies providing goods to the retailers have been among the most ardent RFID resistors, as they fail in general to grasp any real savings from their cooperation. In the center of this tug-of-war, RFID technology has some significant hurdles to overcome. More investments are needed by more participants, even though some of those investments may be obsolete as the technology evolves. More tests and pilots are called for to substantiate the savings for suppliers and retailers. Our stance is clear. Both constituents should now be at work — making careful investments in limited infrastructure and leased solutions, to establish the true costs and benefits, for the time when RFID applications will be pervasive.

In this chapter, we begin our analysis of the retail sector and consider the two strongest reasons behind the drive for RFID acceptance: labor and theft. Both factors have been a part of retailing for centuries, but the adverse publicity associated with what is often considered petty crime and the aversion to labor cutbacks keeps these issues behind the scenes, with greater attention given to inventory management and controlling out-of-stocks. But consumers pay for the excesses and unwarranted losses that can be avoided. With a better understanding of what is at stake, the resistance can be mitigated. From the two major issues, we then move directly to what other factors are at work driving the unstoppable introduction of novel RFID devices into the retail supply chain.

RETAILERS FACE A DIFFICULT BUSINESS FACT

Those in the retail world face a tough business situation every day. In spite of years of effort and the latest in surveillance and security technology, a typical retailer loses 4 to 5 or more percent of revenues to theft and inventory shrinkage each year. That cost is often double what the retailer clears at the end of a year in the form of profits. Various estimates peg the overall cost of fraud, theft, and inventory loss at about $30 billion for U.S. retailers, with the true cost probably somewhat higher due to the inability to come up with actual figures.

It seems employees in the stores; those handling loading, unloading, and shipment; friends who expect special treatment at cash registers; and those simply using the store as a convenient place to get goods without paying are prone to take what they want when the urge strikes. Nearly half of all shrinkage is attributable to employee theft, meaning the problem starts at home. Shoplifting accounts for another 30 percent of the losses, administrative errors another 15 percent, and vendor fraud the final 5 percent. It is a difficult situation, one in which the retailer must cover the cost by passing it on in the price of goods sold. That means the consumer essentially pays for all of the losses. It is a business problem crying out for solution.

Retailers have been attempting to fight the problem with a number of improved technologies. Digital recorders instead of analog tape helped store owners retain a video record of all transactions. New software allows retailers to use computers to link the video with point-of-sale information, eliminating hours of manual search effort to isolate a suspicious transaction. More secure smart cards and biometric security devices are another positive step. Aiding the effort has been the movement to minute, passive microchips and the application of Auto-ID to conceal a powerful message sender within a product or its packaging.

Retailers are on the verge of being able to track items from cradle to grave, as they move from supplier through storage and distribution and eventually to stores. With RFID, retailers will be able to scan a store inventory in a matter of hours, even during store operating hours. The bulky and hardly invisible door sensors that are now being used could be eliminated, replaced with an out-of-sight scanner, which will record each item leaving the store. Linked to the point-of-sale system, it will know immediately which items have been paid for and what has been misappropriated.

Because so much data can be stored on the RFID chips, a scan will immediately identify where the item was purchased, at what price, and by what type of payment. This information gives the retailer the added advantage of catching those people who would return items they purchased with a stolen or illegitimate credit card or without payment of any type. In a successful example, a video rental firm developed an RFID system and used it in conjunction with a drop box, which logged the time the movie was returned through a scanner. By accident, the firm discovered that certain employees were loaning movies to friends without charge. With the RFID devices, the firm quickly discovered which returned items had never been rented and put a stop to the practice.

New hang tags that beep if an item is removed from a garment, digital videos with sharper images that instantly relay store information, and more detailed object identification are among the other techniques under test as retailers continue to make progress with their personal war on crime. Expect to see smaller, lighter, undetectable tags with floor-to-ceiling readers, and look for the readers to achieve commonality to the point where a stolen item will set off an alarm in any store in a shopping mall or within a chain of stores, not just the store where the item was obtained. Overall, we see a better paper trail, with personal shopkeeper identification every time an item's tag is disabled.

WHAT'S DRIVING WAL-MART?

The most notoriety surrounding the RFID technology movement has, of course, been centered on the world's largest retailer. Wal-Mart has always been on the forefront of demanding better identification across its supply chain and was one of the early endorsers of bar coding. It has been leading the charge toward RFID as well, convening a two-day meeting with its top 100 suppliers in Bentonville, Arkansas in November 2003 to construct and announce its game plan. Beginning with the 100 top suppliers, the attendees were told to start with individual case and pallet tagging for shipments starting January 1, 2005. All other suppliers were told to begin shipping RFID-tagged cases and pallets beginning January 1, 2006. Item-level tagging to be read on the shelf would wait until issues with performance, cost, and privacy were resolved. Hardware, software, and integration technology providers attended this groundbreaking session as well and began to understand their role in the process.

Because of the costs and privacy concerns voiced over subsequent tests and compliance, Wal-Mart has modified its aggressive plans, but remains committed to the course of action. Beginning in Texas, and limiting early applications to back rooms and distribution centers, the firm has moved inexorably forward. So what drives such a fierce ambition? Is it the desire to be considered the forerunner in new technology adoption? Or is there a more fundamental factor at work? Retail analyst Stanford C. Bernstein pointed to the more compelling reason when he estimated that "Wal-Mart could save $8.35 billion annually by using RFID — mostly in labor costs from not having to manually scan the bar codes of incoming goods" (Boyle 2003, p. 46).

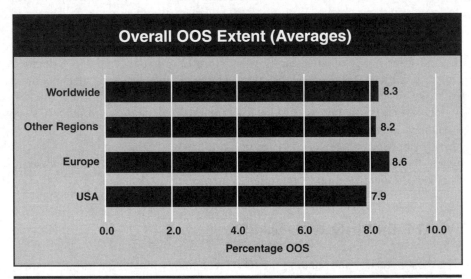

Figure 7.1. Retailing Out-of-Stock Losses: A Typical Retailer Loses About 4 Percent of Sales Due to Out-of-Stocks (Source: 2002 Retail Out-of-Stocks Study by Groen, Corsten, and Bharadway)

For a company that makes about $11 billion a year in net income on sales that keep escalating toward $300 billion, this potential improvement is worthy of much effort and resistance to pushback. But let's start on the top line to see what is really driving Wal-Mart to stay the RFID course. To begin, Figure 7.1 shows that reliable estimates of lost revenues for a retailer due to out-of-stocks can be anywhere from a few percent to 8 or more percent. If a typical retailer loses about 4 percent of sales due to being out of stock, the improvement to the top line for Wal-Mart could be $12 billion in additional revenues. At a 5 percent return on those revenues, the profit could be $600 million annually. This, of course, is the possible return for the largest retailer, but similar order-of-magnitude improvements could be made by any retailer suffering from the cited problems.

Other potential areas of benefit for Wal-Mart are illustrated in Figure 7.2, where we see theft reduction coming close to the advantage to be gained from eliminating out-of-stock conditions. Warehouse item tracking could provide another $300 million, and better inventory control might contribute $180 billion. While any of these numbers is significant and would drive many retailers toward adoption of a controversial technology, the compelling figure is the potential labor savings of $6.7 billion. The total comes close to verifying the Bernstein estimate and serves to substantiate why Wal-Mart and its military imitator are so strongly behind moving RFID toward full-scale adoption.

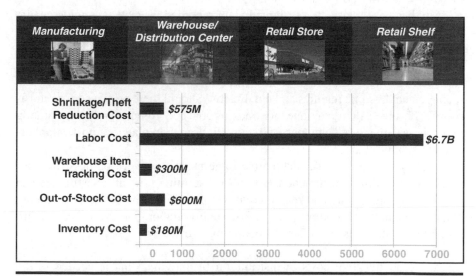

Figure 7.2. Wal-Mart's Anticipated RFID Benefits

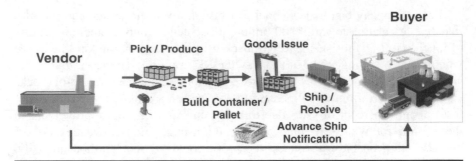

Figure 7.3. End-to-End Support for the Retail Supply Chain

OPPORTUNITIES SPAN THE RETAIL SUPPLY CHAIN

Setting aside the impetus from two giants, there are other reasons for adoption across the end-to-end supply chain processing. If we consider the typical supplier-to-retailer supply chain, as depicted in Figure 7.3, we can see opportunities at each process step or point of handoff. Beginning at the supplier factory or area of distribution, tags can be used to validate what has been packaged, beginning the fight against shrinkage. As the cases are stored for later picking and packing, the documentation continues. As customized pallet loads are built for distribution to the buyer, monitoring moves with the products and remains in contact across the extended enterprise.

Any business transaction is immediately recorded, as well as any losses that might occur. Advance Shipping Notices are prepared and delivered, helping the forecasting and planning part of the process. As goods pass through any further receiving area, they are accurately recorded and any additional information recorded and kept in storage on the chips. Activity recording, reporting, and management become realities and not dreams. Should there be a need for returns or rework, the system continues its tracking and recording, eliminating among other issues the large amount of reconciliation that plagues most supplier-retailer supply chains.

In truly advanced and collaborative systems, the network parties can work together across this fulfillment scenario to determine how all constituents can improve the processing and reap mutual benefits. Since the endgame is supply chain efficiency and bottom-line profits, such collaborative efforts can return hundreds of millions of dollars in operating profits by:

- Reducing total costs of distribution by moving what is needed to the point of need in the right quantities at the right time

- Focusing on shelf landed costs to eliminate extra stocks, always having the right goods on display, and avoiding obsolescence
- Finding innovative uses for the technology, that could eliminate shrinkage without disturbing the cry for privacy
- Immediately shelf stocking the right product at the right time versus relying on periodic stocking schedules, thus improving customer service and reducing lost sales due to out-of-stocks
- Facilitating outsourcing of distribution functions and facilities without loss of important data
- Enabling self-distribution capabilities
- Enabling vendor-managed inventory

As described in Figure 7.4, improving the processes that occur in a merchandising cycle can only serve to improve profits. Buyers and suppliers need to come closer together to develop the true potential of RFID technology, by expanding beyond the obvious gains to labor and theft. From improvements to vendor purchasing plans that result in better sales forecasts and more complete financial planning, the sharing of merchandise plans and special event information can only help all players across the network to improve operating costs and better satisfy the ultimate consumer. With ever-increasing accuracy and data analysis of actual consumer purchases, the avenue is opened for all parties to determine how to increase turnovers and flows across the system.

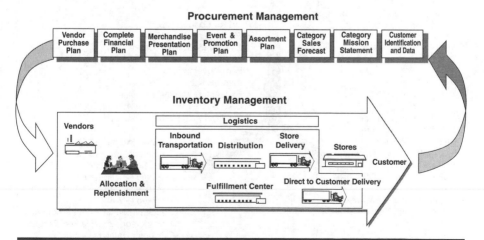

Figure 7.4. Improving Processes and Systems in the Merchandising Cycle Improves Profits

Our viewpoint under these conditions is to use collaboration as a tool for RFID development. Working with a small group of trusted business allies to construct a meaningful supply chain scenario, RFID can be approached first as an improvement to the processing and then as an enabling technology. The players should take a holistic look at their operations to identify the opportunities and consider how RFID will complete the process steps and create best possible performance.

This search begins with improving the return on assets (working capital employed or avoided in inventory) to eliminate aging and obsolescence, to reduce shrinkage, and to limit the need for returns. How RFID can facilitate product traceability and help with any recalls will yield an area of hidden savings. Improvements to cash conversion cycles, elimination of piracy or counterfeiting, improved channel distribution discipline to eliminate wait times and reshipments, and a host of other considerations come into play, as the business constituents begin seeking out the real savings instead of worrying over start-up and implementation costs.

The breakthrough benefits of RFID in the retailing sector are not going to come from the mandates issued by a few giants. They will eventually derive from deep studies of what can be impacted by having greater visibility into the supply chain network that affects retail delivery. That effort begins by considering the impact on the value disciplines described in Figure 7.5. If RFID is truly going to have a positive impact on the retail sector, it should improve a firm's value discipline. That means if a firm is driven by operational excellence,

Product Leadership
- Private Label Products
- Electronic Signing/ Kiosks
- Plan-o-grams
- Item Development
- Item Testing
- Exhaustive Market Shopping
- CAD Systems
- Quality Testing Labs

Operational Excellence
- Warehouse Management
- Electronic Receiving
- Automated Replenishment
- VMI and CFAR
- Quick Response/ECR
- Store Operations
- Communications Networks
- Transportation Networks

Customer Intimacy
- Category Management
- Mass Customization
- Learning Relationships
- e-Marketing and e-Merchandising
- Targeted e-Mail
- Customer Management Programs
- Salesperson Effectiveness Programs
- Customer Databases

Figure 7.5.   Breakthrough Results Should Aid Business Values

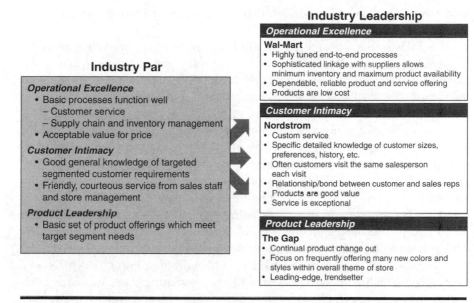

Figure 7.6. Retail Industry Value Disciplines

as is a Wal-Mart, it will concentrate on the possible enhancements to warehouse management and efficiency, improved electronic sensing and receiving, and how to improve automatic replenishment without reliance on possible weak sales forecasts. It means using RFID as a direct enhancement to vendor-managed inventory and collaborative forecasting and replenishment systems. Quick responses are better enabled, as well as efficient consumer responses. Most importantly, store operations are improved as the communication and transportation networks are bringing what the consumer wants at the time of need.

Continuing the analysis is facilitated with a view of Figure 7.6. If a firm is more concerned with customer intimacy, much as a Nordstrom or Bloomingdale's, another set of considerations comes into view. Now the partners work together on improving category management so the consumer never is disappointed, and there is a feeling of customization in the delivery of the specially desired products and services. Retention of knowledge regarding the purchasing process helps the learning relationships with the best customers and aids in any e-marketing and e-merchandising effort. Targeted e-mails, which are proving to be very successful when backed with customer-specific preference data, can be improved with the accuracy and abundance of information that future RFID chips will carry. Special customer programs can be formulated and executed with higher overall results. In short, the customer databases so important for this type of orientation will be enhanced and used for greater sales effectiveness.

Take this scenario a step further and imagine the direct marketing potential if a retail chain used RFID-enabled "smart loyalty cards" that activated when the customer entered the store. Imagine this retail location with the intelligence to identify the customer, query the customer's purchasing history, look up current promotions, and power in-store displays targeted to that customer. This scenario becomes all the more real with the emergence of liquid crystal display (LCD) active tags that can be used in place of price tags on high-value merchandise or shelf price stickers. These LCD "price stickers" communicate via the current wireless (802.11b) network most stores already have installed. In this scenario, "one-to-one" marketing takes on a new life.

A further extension of this type of direct customer connection can be found in the last product developments and R&D efforts of cell phone manufactures. Nokia has already introduced an embedded RFID reader in a cell phone that can act as a credit card. The Near Field Communication Forum led by Nokia, Sony, Royal Philips Electronics, and others is exploring ways in which intelligent devices (e.g., cell phones) can communicate with other intelligent devices (e.g., your car, PC, point-of-sale kiosks, etc.). Awareness of these emerging developments should be incorporated in the firm's long-term strategy for RFID deployment, adoption, and exploitation.

When the firm has oriented its value discipline around product leadership, like a Gap or Victoria's Secret, the effort turns to using RFID as an assist with private label products and the kind of efforts that are needed to always stay ahead of the competition in the introduction of new and successful offerings. Here the enhanced data are used for better product development, shorter cycle times from idea to commercial acceptance, exhaustive joint marketing analysis, and quality testing. With the amount of specific knowledge that RFID can bring to linked development systems and computer-aided design and manufacturing, a new vista is ushered into an environment more typified by mistrust than the possibility for collaborative improvement effort.

WHERE TO LOOK FOR FURTHER OPPORTUNITIES

A host of potential areas appear when collaborative teams are dispatched to pursue improvements across an extended supply chain. Our experience indicates fruit can be found by reducing the need for data capture labor and back office functions. Improvements can be found in better returns from planning and execution systems by feeding them more accurate real-time data. Customer service levels invariably improve. To summarize the potential areas of improvement, there should be:

- Reductions in both inventory and safety stocks needed to maintain high fill rates and eliminate out-of-stocks
- Better cross-docking percentages as the demand information becomes more accurate
- Less costs due to warranty and repair as RFID identifies the point of problem and eliminates false claims
- Reduction in emergency shipments and high-cost overnight and air freight
- Reduction in theft and shrinkage
- Significant reduction in direct labor costs within distribution centers
- Additional applications for RFID technology to identify channel diversion and movement of illegal products
- Improved antitheft capability
- Improved order accuracy and fill rates
- Better seasonal planning and execution as data are tracked closer to events
- Reduction in product deductions

HARDWARE TECHNOLOGY: DON'T OVERLOOK THE PHYSICS

Reaching the scenario we are painting, of course, requires a lot of improvements that are not now present, but are fast approaching. Major players like IBM, Sun, SAP, Philips, and Texas Instruments are involved in the various areas of deployment in RFID technology. From application providers to data management, hardware and readers, and the basic chips and tags, an impressive list of companies are hard at work trying to refine the physics of the process.

RFID is not a "one-size-fits-all" type of development, of course. Rather, what, how, and when an item is tagged makes a difference in performance. In Chapter 10, we will detail the various factors and physics involved in a successful RFID proof-of-concept and pilot, but the following are some of the more important issues that should be considered:

- You (or your selected RFID evaluation partner) will need to develop a testing methodology that examines and captures the relevant performance characteristics, such as read distance, read rate, and optimum tag placement.

■   You will need to test a variety of tags on your products to determine which tag has the best performance. It is likely that no one tag will have the desired performance across your entire product offering.

■   While identifying the optimum tag position, keep in mind the real world of day-to-day operations. It is not realistic to instruct shipping personnel to "carefully place the RFID label 4.5 inches from the leading edge of the pallet and no more than 2.75 inches from the upper edge of the pallet."

■   Every RFID hardware vendor is bound by the same laws of physics. If you understand some of the key principles of RFID engineering, you will gain the ability to sort out product hype from true performance. For instance, the larger the antenna (either on the tag or the receiving antenna), the more likely you will get better read distances and read rates. This is why handheld readers (smaller internal antennas) must be much closer to read a tag than fixed antennas normally found located in dock doors.

RFID Journal and the RFID Alliance Lab (a joint effort of the Information and Telecommunications Technology Laboratory at the University of Kansas and Rush Tracking Systems, a Kansas City area systems integrator) recently published the first in a series of independent tests of commercially available RFID tags. This is an excellent resource to use in beginning to develop the components of your RFID proof-of-concept.

Figure 7.7 depicts the various process points at which data are required and can be collected via RFID technology. From the retail customer order to the manufacturer, through all of the intermediate steps back to the retail shelf, there is a need to capture event information and to update all movements and transactions. So as not to portray too positive a picture of the potentials offered by RFID in retailing and other supply chain sectors, we should point out some remaining complications across such a network. Water absorbs or attenuates a radio frequency, for example, and metal absorbs or reflects radio frequency. Successful applications across the spectrum illustrated must consider the physics of the application as more and more retailers expand globally.

The tag technology must pay attention to the chip and silicon capabilities or the possibilities offered by alternative materials. Frequencies, antenna requirements, and mounting conditions come into the overall picture. As part of the hardware architecture design, on-site assessments must be performed to determine what if any environmental factors are present which would affect the radio frequency signal from an RFID system. This assessment should take into account the presence of electric fans near dock doors, the availability of power

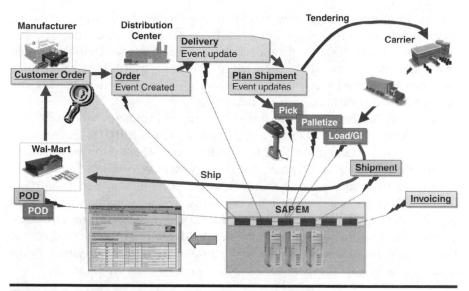

Figure 7.7. Tracking Containers in a Supply Chain

and network supply, type of building materials used, as well as system instal-lation issues (e.g., whether the dock door antennas can be protected from dam-age without decreasing their performance).

We expect these and other complications to be overcome as the technology moves forward. As an example of a successful application, a major retailer that wanted to understand if RFID could deliver improvements commissioned a pilot test involving the technology in a specific range within its environment. The firm selected distribution operations from distribution centers to a chosen group of retail stores. The categories covered by the study included fine jewelry and high-value electronics, such as digital cameras and camcorders. The proposed solution was designed as an on-site RFID test lab to evaluate a wide range of suppliers of tags, readers, and antennas with baseline targeted business objec-tives. An RFID test scenario was developed for each business process. Suppliers included Avery Denison, Tyco, Alien, Symbol, and Intermec. The targets in-cluded improved inventory visibility, reduced shrinkage, elimination of unnec-essary labor, and better asset visibility and control.

The results were positive. The test validated that RFID can yield significant gains to the retailer's business. Significant savings were identified at the dis-tribution center using RFID to capture and eliminate excess handling and reduce damage in white goods (large appliances such as washers, dryers, and refrigerators) handling. In the jewelry area, there were reduced inventory counts and increased delivery efficiencies. Before RFID, cycle counts were required every two hours; with RFID at the item level, these cycle counts were eliminated and sales associate time could be redirected to customer service. In the high-value electronics area, there was increased inventory visibility, reductions in theft, and improvements to customer service ratings.

This proof-of-concept was designed not only to explore new business processes enabled by RFID but also to determine which RFID hardware (tags, antennas, and readers) offered the best performance. Great effort was made to ensure that all variables affecting tag performance were isolated in order to ensure that the results were objective. Once the performance testing was completed and results analyzed, the optimum hardware configuration was installed in order to gather information on how RFID could improve current processes. The results from these tests will be used to develop the business case and limited-scale implementation plan for an RFID-enabled tracking system for the white goods supply chain, with a potential savings of $10 million.

SUPPLY CHAIN VISIBILITY AND EVENT MANAGEMENT

Since nearly 40 percent of all merchandise in a typical retail store is sold under some type of discounted arrangement, special events and trade promotions figure largely into the retail environment. In that area, RFID has another role to play. As we consider supply chain visibility, it will help to differentiate between that factor and event management packages. *Supply chain visibility* is the capture and reporting of information regarding the location and status of product throughout the extended supply chain network. This product can be at rest in a storage facility or moving via various modes of transportation from one location to another and can be independent of who actually owns the product. *Supply chain event management* is the use of this visibility information to react to changing situations. This could be as simple as supporting a special sales event or realizing an inventory level has reached a reorder point, or as complex as redirecting a shipment while in transit to a customer that needs an emergency replenishment.

As seen in Figure 7.8, supply chain event management is a complex process, but solutions help enterprises manage this complexity across extended supply chains and achieve greater operational profitability with virtual command and control. The event management layer captures *internal* and *external* information that will allow the organization to better manage and react to changes. By being able to see inventories and progress of movements through the supply chain, it is easier to maintain customer satisfaction, manage inventories and asset

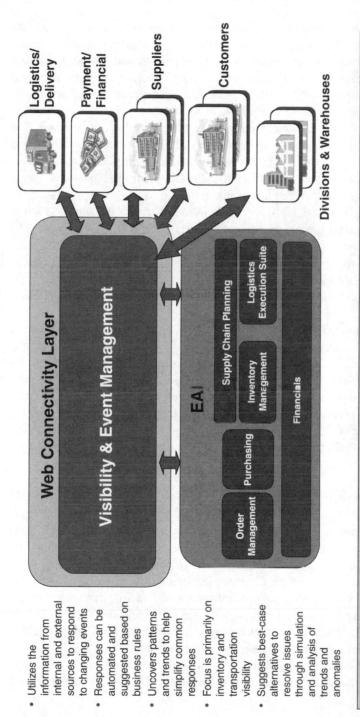

- Utilizes the information from internal and external sources to respond to changing events
- Responses can be automated and suggested based on business rules
- Uncovers patterns and trends to help simplify common responses
- Focus is primarily on inventory and transportation visibility
- Suggests best-case alternatives to resolve issues through simulation and analysis of trends and anomalies

The near future of supply chain execution systems is not a single, integrated application but a heterogeneous set of applications tied together with enterprise application integration and supported with supply chain event management capabilities. These systems allow outside partners a limited view into a company's supply chain

Figure 7.8.   Supply Chain Event Management

utilization, make better purchasing decisions, and control the flow of materials throughout the extended supply chain. Utilization of this information can be through effective business processes or through rules-based system-to-system activities with human intervention for exceptions. It does require an increased level of collaboration as well as stronger internal infrastructure supported with a clear and precise automated identification system.

A leading personal computer manufacturer offers an illustrative story. The firm had an objective to provide visibility into current inventory positions and expected availability across it sales, product management, planning, manufacturing, and customer service functions, in order to synchronize business operations and sales activities. The approach taken was to identify the process, technology, organizational, and application requirements across the business while documenting expected functionality requirements by specific user group. The company developed a solution application architecture that could be blended with legacy systems, an expected upgrade path, and corporate IT directions. A team was set up to establish the IT and business processes and rules for management and maintenance of the solutions, as well as develop training materials and trained users.

The results included a web-based inventory visibility tool that consolidated a number of data sources and provided essential inventory, pricing, life cycle, transition, and forecast information across the business. This enhanced knowledge was used to support key sales, management, and planning objectives. The initiative produced a realized reduction in obsolete inventory and sales order backlog (from 12 percent to 3 percent) and overall inventory reduction from six weeks to four weeks. The order cycle time was improved as well due to better focused sales of available inventory (26 days to 11 days).

PROGRESS IN EUROPE

Supply Chain Management Review estimated in its January/February 2005 issue that 35 percent of European retailers were experimenting with RFID technology, and nearly half of the retailers were planning to conduct pilot efforts in the next year, with 89 percent planning to use some form of RFID by 2006. With a greater emphasis on customer satisfaction than seen in the United States, several European companies are preparing the groundwork to track millions of garments from warehouse to retail outlets using systems developed by DHL Solutions, ASK, and systems integrator NBG-ID. As an example, "Every store of Veronique Delachaux tagged their returns and sent pieces to the logistics warehouse in Marne La Vallee [France] to be inventoried and redirected according to the shipping instructions from the customer," according to DHL's Stephanie Dardanne (www.contactlessnews.com/library/2005/02/28/dhls-garment-rfid-systems/).

Three other major European retailers are pursuing the opportunities offered by RFID technology. Marks & Spencer Group plc is a $15.9 billion retailer that has nearly 400 stores across the United Kingdom. At nine of these stores, customers have been trying on suits bearing RFID tags. The retailer intends to extend usage of these tags to women's lingerie and clothing in 53 stores. According to James Stafford, head of RFID at Marks and Spencer, "RFID, used to tag and identify individual items, is the one technology that can make a dramatic and rapid improvement to customer service in our stores." Laurie Sullivan, from *Information Week,* elaborates: "Without the item-level tracking being tested, it's nearly impossible for the company to keep up to date with 100% accuracy on items that come in complex sizes, such as bras, which have 68 size variations. That results in frustration for the customer who can't find her size in stock" (Sullivan 2005g).

The use of RFID technology is moving relentlessly across Europe, but perhaps with no greater emphasis than in the retail sector. Retailers are pushing the technology beyond pallets and cases to gain the greatest advantage at the store level, with an eye on helping consumers while enhancing sales. Tesco plc has its test store in Leicester, England tracking hundreds of RFID-tagged DVDs, using shelf-mounted readers. In Germany, Metro Group AG, which has been previously cited, has completed tests of RFID-enabled checkout systems at two of its Kaufhof department stores. Signals alert store clerks to restock shelves as the cash registers indicate tagged garments from designer Gerry Weber have been purchased.

These three retailers have a series of initiatives under way with passive RFID tags attached to pallets, cases, and containers. They are fast developing systems to track goods from the time they leave a manufacturing facility until they arrive at the store receiving docks and then onto the racks and into the hands of the consumers. Wal-Mart may be leading the race to get RFID tagging started, but it appears the Europeans are ahead of the game in terms of affixing tags at an item level. "Wal-Mart has been a more cost-conscious and bottom-line driven organization than most European retailers when it comes to RFID," says Christine Overby at Forrester Research. "Wal-Mart has nothing that approaches Metro's Innovation Center, where Metro is testing advanced applications such as an RFID-enabled garment sorter" (Sullivan 2005g). The Innovation Center is located within the firm's warehouse in Neuss. Metro is also testing RFID readers in dressing rooms to scan tags from the clothes being tried on, analyze the information, and search for other available sizes, colors, and complementary accessories, which can be flashed onto a display screen in the room.

Marks & Spencer has also disclosed plans to expand its item-level tracking at the item level. The firm is working with Paxar Corporation, a merchandising and label systems supplier, to develop a "5-inch paper label that will integrate the RFID chip and bar code in the same label. The chips, which will store serial numbers unique to each product, are from EM Microelectronics-Marin SA. Clerks will take inventory at the end of each day by scanning the RFID chips on items remaining on the floor with 868-MHz handheld readers" (Sullivan 2005g). Clerks at stores where these efforts are being tested have been instructed to offer customers the option of having the tags removed in the stores. Tesco has been working with its suppliers in an attempt to move the technology to small items like cosmetics and DVDs, where early results indicate Tesco may have achieved a 4 percent increase in DVD sales — gaining a return on investment within one year.

CONCLUSIONS

Where is it? How many do I have on the shelf? What's in the back room, distribution center, or in transit? These are just a few of the questions that drive the retailer to develop new methods of improving product visibility. For suppliers, case after case study has proven that improved knowledge concerning demand and, most importantly, the ability to quickly respond to demand signals improve profitability. While great improvements in trading partner processes, systems, and software have been made over the past decades, the availability of accurate, real-time product data remains at the core of supply chain inefficiencies. Many of the proponents of RFID see the technology as the solution to this problem. RFID, whether at the item, case, or pallet level, can fulfill the promises offered by an intelligent supply chain.

Imagine supply matching demand, customers finding the products they want when they need them, no labor expense to locate product, no wasted effort in reconciling shipment errors, no product spoilage, and no product shrinkage. These are just a few of the benefits that RFID can deliver to the retailer when it is deployed as an enabling technology to improve supply chain visibility.

8

RFID IN
OTHER SECTORS:
TECHNOLOGY
ACCEPTANCE
OR REJECTION

From security and military implementations to retailers and health care providers, applications for RFID are appearing weekly. In a seemingly relentless way, new possibilities are being discovered, developed, and applied. By now, each reader has undoubtedly made use of one form of RFID or another — passing through a tollbooth on the highway, using a smart card to buy gasoline or burgers, entering a building with an RFID access card, or participating in a retail payment system. Across the world, other countries are entering the game as well. Prepaid electronic money, using contactless auto-identification technology, has been in effect for the euro and yen. You can use both at retail shops and for cyberspace shopping, charging from credit cards or using cash. British Petroleum is applying identification and location information supplied by RFID on its large tanker ships, to check temperatures through sensors placed on cases of food and produce. BP is also tracking the state of its people and assets, discovering where a pump might be stuck or an air-conditioning unit not working. Reduced insurance and maintenance costs are among the benefits, as well as better conditions on board the ships that are subject to lengthy voyages.

The "Octopus Card" is a single smart card used to pay all the fares on underground trains, ferries, buses, and light rail in Hong Kong since September 1997. The goal in that country is to grow nontransport purchases from 10 percent now to 50 percent. In a similar vein, access control cards are gaining acceptance, used for entry, verifying credentials, ticketing, and automatic turnstile applications at sports and media events. Texas Instruments is a leading producer of these cards.

Chep, the world's leading producer of pallets and container pooling services, is hard at work helping to facilitate the RFID transformation. This firm has decided to create information value for its customers by enabling them to track assets using RFID technology. The firm has designed a customized RFID pallet tag, which is capable of long read ranges and can work with sophisticated forklift truck readers, portal readers, and conveyor commissioning (inspection) systems. The company expects to reduce product damage and reduce customer shrinkage with better tracking, while improving cycle times from use to return.

From another aspect, there is almost no limit to how far the technology and similar techniques can go, sometimes approaching an Orwellian world of control. We should point out that the original name for an RFID reader was Interrogator. The concept is that the tag will give up all of its information when it is powered up or authenticated by an authorized reader. In Israel, cross-ID and Nanotags are being used; these microscopic chemical tags, with an anonymously long read range, can be inserted in any material, organic or inorganic, and not be seen (they can see you) by an observer. Invisible supermarket tagging within packaging itself from Inkode is also under test. Ceramic bolus RFID tags, a little larger than a grain of rice, can be injected under the skin for longer use. A group of doctors has considered implanting a tiny identifying tag in the foot of each newborn baby to track location through a lifetime. One doctor who is an avid skier implanted a tag in his shoulder so he could be tracked in case of avalanche or becoming disoriented or lost in a snowstorm. At one hospital in Mexico, doctors are implanting a similar chip in newborns, to combat the child abduction problem in that country.

The future of RFID certainly includes the blending of speed pass tokens, prepaid smart cards, and retail payment systems into a complete financial transaction system, without banks or other financial institutions. In Asia, you can expect to see a steady rise in the use of RFID contactless or no-contact smart cards, for payments outside of transportation. In this chapter, we will investigate just how far the RFID technology might proceed, as we look at applications in other industries and peek into areas from pharmaceuticals and health services to tires, metal processing, and land vehicle systems. As we do, we will once again pay tribute to the advocates and cynics supporting or inhibiting the movement.

ENABLING INTERNAL/EXTERNAL INTEGRATION

Successful RFID tests are appearing in a wide variety of places. In Chapter 5, we reported that RFID tags are being used in a planned real-time network application that will continuously monitor hazardous chemicals stored in five National Aeronautics and Space Administration (NASA) facilities at Edwards Air Force Base in southern California. The network, which NASA implemented in 2005, detects and reacts to break-ins, chemical thefts, and dangerous spills. Dubbed ChemSecure, it will "replace antiquated standalone systems that transmit information to separate databases and departments" (Sullivan 2005b, p. 21).

Such applications are a result of ongoing efforts in the RFID technology arena. To begin, messaging and enterprise application integration middleware systems have been available for some time to convert information from various sources into updates to management systems. Technical architectures have been mapped out to evaluate packages in order to better understand the infrastructure to support specific applications. RFID simply becomes an enhancement to the data collection part of such systems — a means to speed real-time access to more accurate information.

Understanding the business requirements and desired use of the information gathered is essential to focus any meaningful development and selection criteria. Companies should be at work developing the relationships they want to enhance, creating systems to provide cleaned and accurate data and tightly integrated systems, between their internal processes and external business networks, before they move to advanced levels of supply chain management systems.

Consider the situation faced by the Coca-Cola Company. Using RFID technology with wireless communication, the firm can collect primary data from its vending machines. The number of sales by product type can be accessed from a handheld device. The total cash and refund data can be gathered, with individual product line price and any out-of-stock information. The database managing system can alert managers, dispatch assistance, prepare technical and performance reports, and integrate the information in back office systems. The early results indicate an 18 to 23 percent net profit lift due to improved inventory management, fewer stock-outs, faster repairs, and efficient routing of delivery drivers.

Other opportunities that have appeared include:

- **Supply chain application architecture** — The ability to assess the functions to be performed across an end-to-end system and evaluate the current applications for the ability to perform those functions in order to build a framework for managing supply chain activities more effectively

- **Enterprise application integration** — The capability to establish intra-enterprise connectivity and data sharing (i.e., defining how applications will work together, to share knowledge quickly and efficiently, preventing much of the errors and problems found in current supply chain processing)
- **Business process development** — Defining detailed responses to key events whether the response will be supported by systems integration or through human interaction, raising the level of effectiveness of these events and reducing the cycle times
- **Organizational infrastructure development** — Determining how to structure the organization around supply chain applications and react to the information provided by these new capabilities

In contemporary supply chain systems, external supply chain partners are among the key providers of data, so any communication system must be global and capable of processing real-time data. Identifying the few important links in a supply chain and developing relationships using RFID technology with those firms will pay dividends in the form of more timely and accurate visibility of orders and shipments. Consider how a major automobile manufacturer is applying RFID technology to the tracking of tires. Ford is using a system to write U.S. Department of Transportation information to the tires at the point of manufacture. The system then tracks the tires to storage and assembly on a car with a specific vehicle identification number (VIN). At a later time, the same system can provide information to verify mounting or to verify the VIN and the tire data, after tire installation. This solution can help make any tire recalls much less costly by relating tire manufacturing data to the specific vehicle and owner.

Developing collaborative relationships with supply chain partners may not yield immediate results, but it leads to a focused plan for building the wireless communication system of the future before competitors, and thereby taking advantage of the technology ahead of the pack. Achieving such an advantage can be developed from opportunities to use:

- **Partnering diagnostic lab (PDL)** — To determine each supply chain partner's ability or need for learning to collaborate successfully with one or more of the emerging RFID trends. The PDL (described in the Appendix) is a facilitated two-day intense effort to study process maps and draw on RFID expertise across a business network to define solutions that are pertinent to a market or customer segment. With the PDL, potential partners work together to prioritize the development of new capabilities to support their combined goals.

- **Supplier relationship management** — To develop deep collaborative relationships with key suppliers and gain a market advantage through RFID applications. Sharing insights into customer requirements and the need to meet mandates is just the beginning. Ongoing efforts will lead to gaining an advantage as the proactive partners move forward and other firms continue to be stuck in place studying the movement to death.
- **Extended architecture, such as E3** — To build an interenterprise generic framework for the smooth flow of information between applications and business partners, with quick integration and advanced capabilities.

Fundamentally, the first generation of high-volume RFID applications has been in place, broadcasting an object's identification data to an appropriate reader. Subsequent developments will further the ability to embed more information in the readable tags and allow more effective communication between other objects through a wireless environment. In this brave new world of data processing, objects will be enabled to communicate among themselves, creating what amounts to ad hoc processing opportunities to track arrivals, transfers, and consumption. Problems associated with over- or undershipments, misplacement of products, pilferage, tampering, shrinkage, and theft can be subdued. As hardware and software become more robust, a new era is ushered in, producing a seamless environment enhanced with wireless connectivity between the objects, their users, and final consumers.

It becomes what Rajit Gadh, professor at UCLA and head of the Wireless Internet for Mobile Enterprise Collaboration, calls an "Internet of Artifacts." Gadh expects objects to communicate and exchange information to take identity-based actions, creating artifact networks. He predicts that a thorough radio frequency planning step will become a necessary part of any progression toward achieving what becomes a seamless, wireless connectivity system that establishes industrially scalable RFID solutions. In this world, a wide variety of business applications become possible. Let us consider some of the more popular examples being tested or implemented.

RFID MOVEMENTS ARE BECOMING PERVASIVE

A logical question at this point is: Where is the RFID movement going? The answer begins to paint the ubiquitous picture we envision. Companies involved in goods transfer are facing the inevitable. An example is the airline industry, as it comes to grips with the constant problems of misplaced luggage and coping with growing security issues. This industry is hard at work testing and developing a vision of a future without lost luggage and no possibility of transfer of illegal or terrorist activity products. In an effort to ensure safety of lives, McCarran International Airport in Las Vegas has made an investment in 100 million RFID tags to "ensure that all baggage has been through the airport's explosive-detection and screening equipment. The tags will be printed by ticket agents and attached to passengers' bags at ticket counters. Each tag will contain a unique number, as well as passenger information" (Bacheldor 2003b, p. 32). Most businesses that involve suppliers and users still do not have a sufficient level of awareness to substantiate a similar effort, but the mandates continue to drive response, so we anticipate a growing number of such tests and pilots.

Beaver Street Fisheries provides an example of how a firm can use the technology in a proactive manner to build revenues. CIO Howard Stockdale made a decision in early 2004 to use RFID technology to track cases and pallets of fish and more exotic seafood — including alligator and turtle meat — at the company's seafood processing and packing plant. "He bought into RFID to lower costs and improve internal operations, but also hoped he'd convince Wal-Mart Stores Inc. to add the $500 million frozen-fish importer to the list of companies required to meet the retailer's January 2005 RFID-compliance mandate for its top-100 suppliers" (Sullivan 2004a, p. 49).

Beaver Street was granted its wish. While most of the suppliers on the Wal-Mart list had until January 2006 to comply, the fish importer is already qualified. The firm plans to move further and build the technology into systems and business processes to take advantage of the efficiencies it introduces. Small and medium-size companies like Beaver Street are advised to take such a proactive stance and determine how to make RFID work. For its lab testing, Beaver Street has installed RFID readers and plans to include handheld devices. The firm's IT department is rewriting its internal enterprise resource planning system to accommodate the flood of data it expects to result from RFID use.

Suppliers will need to incur much of the development costs, until there is greater documentation of the actual costs and benefits. Then we expect to see more joint efforts to expand usage. Eventually, the costs will be passed on to the end consumer, less the savings from the beneficial improvements. We strongly advise that pilots (to be discussed in Chapter 10) be designed and approached on a proactive basis to identify the missing ingredients and document the actual costs and benefits. The Land Systems case, to be detailed later, was a move in that direction. RFID must be positioned as one tool in the drive for total visibility into the end-to-end supply chain processing, taking its place as an enabler. The ultimate savings will come from this visibility and more than offset the costs, especially as use and scale drive down the costs of the components.

Savings will arrive from many sources and applications. Consider the need to trace accountability for the mad cow disease scare. RFID tagging of cows in Michigan led to the identification of infected cows in a few hours. It took 48 hours and a check on 100 million animals, with tags in their ears enabled with RFID, to conclude that part of the investigation. In contrast, it took two weeks for federal officials to complete the DNA tests that confirmed the Alberta, Canada birthplace of a Washington State cow that was identified on December 23, 2003 as having bovine spongiform encephalopathy, or mad cow disease. The U.S. Department of Agriculture (USDA) had to wade through a mountain of paper records and other data maintained by breeders and meat packers to trace and recall beef that may have been exposed to tissue from the infected cow. Prices for live cattle dropped about 15 percent the week of the discovery. A herd of nearly 450 Holstein calves, among the identifiable offspring of the infected cow, had to be destroyed.

Track and trace for a live animal, from farm to the processing plant, is one of the hot issues being pursued by many organizations. The future is now in the hands of the U.S. Department of Homeland Security, which has taken over much of the USDA's role in cross-border transportation of animals, plants, and soon packaged goods. In a complementary move, the Country of Origin Label (CoOL) is a new worldwide program being introduced from Japan. The U.S. Congress shelved this legislation, but we expect to see it enacted soon. The fact that the mad cow incident involved a Canadian firm of origin makes it a short investigative jump to CoOL programs, instead of going through boycotts and national bans. Expect processor-to-supermarket track and trace to appear as well, possibly in a few more years.

RFID readers are available in a variety of forms to meet a variety of needs. From an industrial aspect, International Paper Company has gone live with a fully automated RFID tracking system. Based on Electronic Product Code (EPC) standards, that firm has replaced bar code system tags with RFID tags embedded in cores of paper rolls, readable through more than six feet of paper. With this enhanced system, the company can track the movement of paper rolls from the point of manufacture through paper distributors or its direct delivery network to the end user, typically other manufacturers that convert the paper into industrial supplies like corrugated boxes, printing paper, multiwall paper sacks, and grocery bags. Where there were instances before in which locations of rolls were temporarily lost, the new system now tracks them from manufacture to point of use.

International Paper has also gone so far as to introduce RFID forklifts. In an effort to reduce the need for RFID readers and portals at each entry point or dock door at its distribution centers, the company developed and introduced

RFID forklifts through its "Smart Packaging" business unit in 2003. The trucks are designed to improve inventory accuracy and reduce the number of lost shipments. The specially equipped trucks can read product code pallet tags and then track movement as the pallets are transferred through a warehouse. The firm claims that customers with RFID systems in place can integrate their infrastructure with the forklifts.

These applications are not without problems, however. Because wireless networks have been found to interfere with in-store readers, more technical work is necessary. Readers are sometimes considered too slow for certain applications like high-speed filling lines, and damage occurs as the users develop experience skills. The U.S. Department of Defense, for example, has yet to endorse any specific technology software provider, and pending legislation in California and Utah could restrict retailers' use of RFID technology. For these and other reasons, technical development must continue and be accelerated. These issues are not showstoppers, but represent hurdles that need to be scaled.

Making supply chain RFID pay off for suppliers and users must become a joint effort. Systems integration is the key cost to control in any implementation of RFID as a solution. Most businesses already have a supply chain enhancement solution in the works, but many are not yet RFID ready. Companies are well advised to be prepared when a customer suddenly requires RFID tags at the case and pallet level. Once RFID data begin to flow, companies need to use the results to verify improvements to order cycle times, inventory quantities and hold times, and logistical costs per tagged container. When at least two RFID-enabled trading partners reach about 50 percent of trade being tagged, inefficiencies in interenterprise visibility and tracking will become apparent. Let's take a look at a specific area of application.

PHARMACEUTICAL APPLICATIONS

The U.S. Food and Drug Administration (FDA) issued its final rules on maintaining food traceability records under the Bioterrorism Act in December 2004. All companies that manufacture and transport food products must maintain records that identify the immediate previous source and subsequent receipt of the food they distribute. Incumbent within the rule is the requirement that bar codes be placed on the labels of drugs and biological products such as blood. At a minimum, the bar code must include each drug's National Drug Code Number. Product manufacturers may include other useful information such as lot number, shipment data, and expiration date.

Although the early portions of the FDA timeline emphasize tracking at the case and pallet level, by late 2007 it is expected that most item-level pharmaceuticals will be tagged as well. With over 12 billion units in the U.S. market, the RFID potential is huge. Tracking and tracing capabilities are now an important aspect for pharmaceutical manufacturers, especially to track product pedigree, facilitate product recalls, or take actions that require following the product through its delivery channel. RFID is particularly suited to coping with the issue of counterfeiting and the layered approach advised by the FDA, including tamperproof packaging, bar codes, and other forms of security like hidden inks.

These techniques are already in use in the pharmaceutical industry, on bottles, blister packs, and aerosol products. They are also being used by a number of manufacturers of blood products intended for transfusion. Typically, the linear bar code specifies the name of the blood-collecting facility, the name and blood type of the donor, and the product number. In hospitals, doctors can feed this data and the product codes of prescribed medication into computers. Through smaller portable computers, nurses administering medications can match the codes of products about to be dispensed with a patient's bar-coded wristband to prevent any mistakes. "Preventable medication errors cause 7,000 deaths in the U.S. each year, according to a widely respected Institute of Medicine report. The *Archives of Internal Medicine* reported approximately one in five doses of medication administered in hospitals and skilled nursing facilities is given in error" (Zebra Technologies 2004, p. 2). In multiple studies, researchers have noted an 80-plus percent reduction in medication errors is possible.

Figure 8.1 provides a generalized view of where the RFID effort is being tested or applied across life science supply chains. In the business sector, suppliers, manufacturers, distributors, and health care providers are working to create specific applications. In the process area, special pilots within factories have been established, and readers are being used in factories, warehouses, and transportation facilities to track and trace movements. This effort extends to distributors that play a key role in total fulfillment in this industry. The loop is completed as readers are showing up in the providers' warehouses and point-of-care areas. The applications listed and more are coming under the microscope to validate actual improvements, along with order-of-magnitude figures for costs and benefits.

Compliance to the FDA mandate and with the Prescription Drug Marketing Act brings a new dimension to life sciences and the pharmaceutical industry as well. Many organizations in life sciences are applying bar coding, RFID, and secure media to comply with FDA rules and customer requests. Calculations

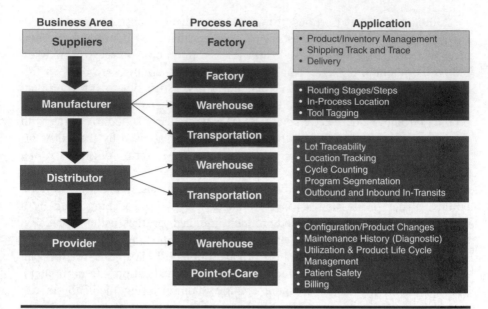

Figure 8.1. Life Sciences Supply Chain Applicability of RFID

by A.T. Kearney in its report "Meeting the Retail RFID Mandates" suggest over-the-counter drug manufacturers can recoup their capital outlays in RFID systems and produce a positive sustainable return on investment in slightly over one year by using the technology for internal inventory control and distribution operations. An Accenture study found that improved visibility from RFID could allow manufacturers to reduce their safety stock by up to 30 percent (Zebra Technologies 2004, p. 5).

CASE STUDY: PURDUE PHARMA

Purdue Pharma provides an action example of what can be accomplished, as described by Mark Roberti in the January/February 2005 issue of *RFID Journal*. Stamford, Connecticut–based Purdue Pharma is known for such over-the-counter medicines as Betadine antiseptics and Senikot laxatives. The firm also makes prescription drugs and narcotics and wanted to track these medications. When Wal-Mart announced it would require suppliers of Schedule II narcotics to tag individual bottles with RFID tags in 2004, senior executives at Purdue "felt RFID was the wave of the future and would eventually deliver benefits throughout the pharmaceutical supply chain by reducing counterfeiting and improving patient safety. They made the bold decision not just to comply with the Wal-Mart mandate, but to integrate RFID into Purdue's OxyContin product line. By doing this, they could capture data as the product moved from its packaging area to 'the vault' — a super-secure storage area — and then to the shipping area" Roberti 2005b, p. 14).

Purdue formed a cross-functional action team and started identifying companies that could deliver RFID tags based on the Class 1 and Class 0 EPC specifications, settling on Matrics (recently acquired by Symbol Technologies). Matrics worked with SAP's supply chain management system to develop a prototype for its facility in Wilson, North Carolina. In April 2004, with the help of its collaborators, Purdue launched a test in which the reader was able to read every serial number on 48 individually tagged bottles packed in cartons 10 feet from the reader antenna. The captured data went to a server at SAP headquarters in Walldorf, Germany and then presented back to the Purdue system.

With this success, the company then began to work with Lebanon, New Hampshire–based NJM/CLI Packaging Systems International to determine what antennas would be placed on the packaging and how the readers would interact with the programmable logic controller that monitors and controls the line. A requirement was that every tag be functioning before and after it was applied to a bottle. The RFID tag also needed to be integrated into the product label off-site, so the label could be applied normally at the packaging site. There also could be no defective tags placed on the bottles, as the cost of removing and replacing would be prohibitive. Guilford Gravure, a label maker from Guilford, Connecticut, designed the system to integrate the tags into labels before shipping those labels to Purdue and to remove those bottles that did not respond to readers from the line. A method for integrating the RFID tags into Purdue's anticounterfeiting features was also included.

After much testing to make sure labels were not damaged in shipment and the packaging line could function in a fail-safe manner, six cases of test placebos were shipped to Wal-Mart, in a pilot intended to match the retailer's requirement that "100 percent of all tags on bottles be readable while the bottles were still in the case." Wal-Mart personnel were able to read every tag. The biggest problem was then to find "a way to integrate RFID into the packaging line without slowing down the process" (Roberti 2005b, p. 16).

Under the system that was developed, a machine feeds exactly 100 pills into each bottle, which travels down a conveyer to be sealed and capped. The tag is read by a reader antenna the size of a paperback book. If that reader does not pick up the EPC number, a burst of air blows the bottle from the line. If the tag is successfully read, a supervisor with a touch-screen computer can enter information about the product and check to make sure the EPC number on the RFID tag has the right product identification. After the tags are read, the bottles are grouped into lots of six, which are shrink-wrapped and placed by hand into small cases that hold a total of 48 bottles each. After eight lots of six bottles are put into a case and sealed with tamperproof tape, they move to another reader where all 48 bottles are read, to compare the serial numbers to make sure there are no duplicate numbers. Then 100 cases are stacked on a pallet and taken to a conveyor where they are again sent under the scrutiny of another reader. The bottles are read and then put into the vault. When they are removed from storage, the bottles are read one more time before being shipped to Wal-Mart's warehouse in Bentonville, Arkansas.

Purdue began its rollout on November 29, 2004 when a small team of executives and packaging, IT, and security experts from the firm went live with the unique system for tagging large numbers of items with EPC tags at its facility in Wilson, North Carolina. The first batch of 20,000 tagged bottles went through successfully. There were only two defective tags, which were kicked off the line. "Long term, we think RFID is the right approach for product authentication and creation of an electronic pedigree throughout the supply chain," says David Richiger, executive director of package design and development (Roberti 2005b, p. 20). Purdue is not planning to stop with this successful application. The firm is installing a second system in its Totowa, New Jersey packaging facility.

There are other expected pharmaceutical and medical device benefits. Figure 8.2 describes pictorially the many steps that extend the life sciences value chain, including cycle times, inventory, and related cost opportunities. Drug anticounterfeiting and authentication have been mentioned, and it is anticipated they will have a major positive impact across the industry, reducing the current annual global supply chain costs of $500 billion. Specimen tracking during drug development will shorten cycle times for approval. Sample drug inventory management during clinical trials should be improved. Medical errors will be reduced, increasing patient safety. Automated replenishment at retailers and hospitals is already under way. Traceability of targeted recalls will be facilitated, helping pharmaceutical companies track drug inventory to ensure drugs are available at doctors' offices.

OTHER INDUSTRY ISSUES AND CHALLENGES

A summary of expected improvements for health care and other industries includes:

- Supply chain efficiency
  - □ Reduced handling costs

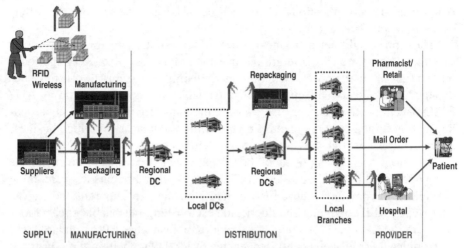

RFID can dramatically reduce cycle time and inventory while improving service delivery

Figure 8.2. RFID in the Life Sciences Supply Chain

- ☐ Lower shrinkage
- ☐ Less out-of-stocks
- ☐ Shipping accuracy
- ☐ Automated receipt and reorder
- ■ Track and trace
  - ☐ Inventory accuracy
  - ☐ Reduce holding of slow and obsolete inventory
  - ☐ Ensure chain of custody
- ■ Product authentication
  - ☐ Ensure authenticity, eliminate piracy and counterfeiting
  - ☐ Real brand versus knockoff
  - ☐ Avoid theft and unauthorized diversion
  - ☐ Reduce recalls

The keys to deploying RFID in health care and other industries fit a framework for execution. The first step is to expand education on the technology and its uses across a business, as our research indicates very limited awareness exists. A source for practical and impartial automatic identification technology (AIT) and RFID expertise should be identified and used. The key is to make certain the business understands RFID and how to develop and leverage the technology across interactive networks within any unique supply chain environment. That requires knowledge of the appropriate hardware, software, and suppliers needed for applications. Care must be taken here to sort out the differences between facts and fiction.

The firm should set a business-process-focused strategy for RFID implementation, complete with a return on investment business plan. Keep the focus on the fundamental impacts of RFID, as the company begins to carefully understand the impacts and opportunities available through integration of AIT/RFID data into existing enterprise resource planning (ERP) systems. In particular, getting started requires identifying the point of departure or which business processes can benefits the most by being RFID enabled with minimal risk.

The need for development of better data standards that allow real-time exchange of useful data regardless of platform, or what amounts to overcoming the rigidity of company-centric ERP systems, becomes an important factor. The next step in RFID planning should include establishing reasonable expectations from any RFID efforts. A company should anticipate that EPC standards will be completed for all levels and frequencies of RFID tags within three years. It can also expect that the ISO frequencies and rules for over-the-air interfaces will be purged of competing devices and signals within two years. Also, it can be expected that the EPC Generation 2 tag will become the standard in widest use and that within five to seven years we should see quantity pricing in the sub-10-cent range.

Passive tag costs (currently at about 30 cents in low volumes), rules for placement, product testing, network bandwidth, scale of production, accuracy of sensing, reader costs, and security/privacy concerns should all improve in the next three years. Learning curves will also improve as the actual costs and benefits beyond compliance are determined. Industry support and pilots will ensue that lead to roadmaps, clarification of costs and responsibilities, and implementation methodologies into supply chains. The results are already being documented, as some serious case studies indicate.

CURRENT APPLICATION IN
AN INDUSTRIAL ENVIRONMENT

As one example, the Land Systems division of defense giant General Dynamics approached compliance to the U.S. Department of Defense unique identification (UID) and RFID mandate in a systematic manner. This firm used the mandate as the compelling event to begin the alignment and improvement of a variety of disparate internal systems, while examining potential improvements in operational efficiencies. That is, it decided to try a test application to meet a mandate and use the test to find out if there was anything in the game for the company. The first step was to establish a multidisciplinary team, with members from General Dynamics' IT and supply chain groups and help from CSC Consulting.

The team examined current product and information in order to first develop a rough order-of-magnitude (ROM) estimate of first-year compliance costs and outline projected expenses over the next five years. This ROM was developed by performing representative site visits to gain an understanding of where and how UID and RFID processes would be implemented. With an understanding of processes affected, the team then began the work of exploring the various alternatives and options available to General Dynamics in terms of hardware and software integration. A decision matrix was agreed upon that would act as a filter for the options considered. Minimizing plant and process disruption, maximizing internal efficiencies, and avoiding duplicate systems were a few of the filters developed.

Through this analysis, the team developed four possible solution paths that included equipment lists, capital cost estimates, timing of efforts, and system integration issues. After weighing the alternatives against the decision matrix, a suitable solution was identified. The solution selected orchestrated deployment of RFID and UID processes with the timing of the U.S. Department of Defense deployment schedule and implementation of a large-scale ERP system. Quick system improvements were selected to bring together the various receiving, shipping, and DD250 submissions required to gain payment for government orders. These improvements would act as a bridge until the ERP system was completely implemented in 2007.

SUMMARY

Combining product identification with other variable information at different packaging levels throughout various industries offers an opportunity to capitalize on RFID technology. Coding and reading, tracking and tracing, and inventory management techniques enhance a supply chain and its ability to respond to customer mandates and bring a new level of savings to the firm. More work is needed to reduce costs and to verify actual benefits, but the move is well under way across the industries we have cited, and more are moving carefully from the sidelines into the action arena.

9

BUILDING THE RFID BUSINESS CASE AND ROADMAP FOR EXECUTION

In a decade, the prediction by advocates is that RFID will be pervasive and linked to massive computer networks, enabling benefits such as faster grocery store checkout, medicine chests that prompt users to take their pills, and refrigerators with milk cartons that call for replacement. The positive outlook extends to eliminating counterfeit drugs and entertainment ware, reducing shrinkage to the point where consumers can see a benefit in retail pricing, preventing the theft of cars, achieving rapid and accurate tracing and tracking of vital materiel needed by our war fighters, and tracing the movement of babies and small children to keep them from harm's way.

The movement is already in progress, with more examples appearing weekly. In each of Ford's 50 U.S. auto parts and assembly plants, woven into the superstructure supporting the roofs are a network of antennas that are receiving radio signals from the factory floor and even from outside the plant. As Dale Buss of *Automotive Logistics* explains, "The signals are being emitted by battery-powered, hand-held RFID pendants....Electronic eye sensors and line workers are signaling that the levels of certain parts are low and must be replenished; a run of vehicles that display the need for rework on a particular body panel are pinging the antenna about where they have been shunted" (Buss 2004, p. 68).

The automaker developed the systems with Santa Clara, California–based WhereNet, using active tags that emit their own signals and very accurate location hardware and software, in one more example of what industries are doing to reap the benefits of RFID technology. In the Ford factories, and at other car manufacturing sites where the emphasis is on lean manufacturing and a premium is placed on efficiency and elimination of waste, RFID is becoming one of the solutions, especially to help the speedy and effective movement of parts and assemblies to the point of need in kanban systems. At a BMW plant in Spartanburg, South Carolina, as each car is being assembled, a two-inch-by-three-inch active tag is attached, signaling the progress of the car throughout the assembly operation, including such manufacturing data as torque settings used for seat attachment.

General Motors has been deploying RFID technology within its European plants to track cars since the 1980s. GM has advanced to deploying radio transmission without ID tags, through its expanding experimentation with wireless transmission zones within its factories, particularly with the use of forklift trucks. Previously, to signal the forklift driver to bring fresh parts to an assembly line, line operators had to punch buttons on a light board that generated a paper ticket that drivers picked up before responding with the needed parts. In the new radio frequency environment, line operators send signals to the radio receivers on the trucks, which are connected to small onboard computers and printers that produce a series of parts requests. "We've cut out 200 miles of forklift travel per shift," reports Ron Gravish, manager of wireless technology for supply chain material flow planning for GM (Buss 2004, p. 70).

Through the preceding chapters, we have described a variety of considerations that could be impacted by what we have painted as an inevitable, pervasive movement toward supply chain visibility and ubiquitous wireless communications, both enhanced by the application of RFID technology. In this chapter, we will proceed with advice on how a business should carefully adopt the technology and use it as an element of a business case for action. RFID should then be built into the firm's business strategy as an enabler of market intentions, to take greatest advantage of this inevitable technology acceptance and deployment.

RFID BUSINESS OPPORTUNITIES ACROSS THE SUPPLY CHAIN

As a firm considers its business plans and how the business can improve performance with RFID technology, it should start with what aspects of the supply chain network can be enhanced — from upstream product tagging to back-end enterprise resource planning integration and downstream customer delivery and satisfaction. Such an analysis requires a focus on which business process improvements will result in a strategic advantage, through attention to the physics of RFID technology, what data will be generated, where and how that data will be captured, how data will be shared, the architecture that will be incorporated into the design, and the aspects of a supply chain that will be improved through deployment. In the process, an enterprise-wide view should be taken, to make certain reasonable risks are involved for the linked constituents and unnecessary expenses and wastes are avoided.

GETTING STARTED REQUIRES
A GUIDING FRAMEWORK

To start RFID planning, Figure 9.1 is used as a reminder of how the technology works and what occurs within the context of a possible future-state supply chain vision. This pictorial is an elaboration over those presented before and is intended to be a generic version of how we see RFID being deployed across many industries and applications. A firm wanting to begin its RFID plan should construct such a process flow framework, so parties involved have a simple but clear picture of what will be evolving. It also serves to bring out any early concerns and points where cynics believe the system could break down. Beginning with RFID technology, tags with an embedded chip will be used to store a unique Electronic Product Code (EPC) to identify the various products entering the construction and delivery system. How much identity there should be on the tag becomes a function of the desired end results by the firm and its business partners. The tag can be either a passive identifier or actively beam a radio signal, so information can be transferred and its specific numbers and identification read. Middleware must be carefully selected to filter the raw data and apply relevant business rules to control what goes into the core systems for a host of business purposes.

Through the Internet, an enterprise transaction system is established with visibility into what is transpiring. Now the radio waves allow the tags to be detected at specific points along the extended supply chain. Object Name Service (ONS) servers match the EPC number from tag-reading events to the address of a specific remote server, providing the members of the EPC network with detailed information about the products, their whereabouts, and progress. After careful testing and consideration, specific company rules can now be applied — to govern access and use of the data, while assuring security among the network members.

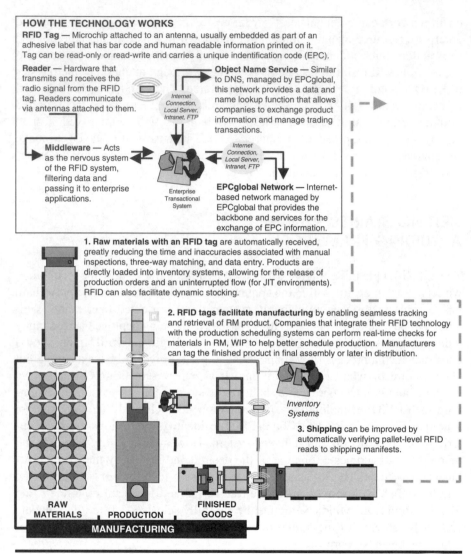

HOW THE TECHNOLOGY WORKS

RFID Tag — Microchip attached to an antenna, usually embedded as part of an adhesive label that has bar code and human readable information printed on it. Tag can be read-only or read-write and carries a unique indentification code (EPC).

Reader — Hardware that transmits and receives the radio signal from the RFID tag. Readers communicate via antennas attached to them.

Internet Connection, Local Server, Intranet, FTP

Object Name Service — Similar to DNS, managed by EPCglobal, this network provides a data and name lookup function that allows companies to exchange product information and manage trading transactions.

Middleware — Acts as the nervous system of the RFID system, filtering data and passing it to enterprise applications.

Internet Connection, Local Server, Intranet, FTP

Enterprise Transactional System

EPCglobal Network — Internet-based network managed by EPCglobal that provides the backbone and services for the exchange of EPC information.

1. Raw materials with an RFID tag are automatically received, greatly reducing the time and inaccuracies associated with manual inspections, three-way matching, and data entry. Products are directly loaded into inventory systems, allowing for the release of production orders and an uninterrupted flow (for JIT environments). RFID can also facilitate dynamic stocking.

2. RFID tags facilitate manufacturing by enabling seamless tracking and retrieval of RM product. Companies that integrate their RFID technology with the production scheduling systems can perform real-time checks for materials in RM, WIP to help better schedule production. Manufacturers can tag the finished product in final assembly or later in distribution.

Inventory Systems

3. Shipping can be improved by automatically verifying pallet-level RFID reads to shipping manifests.

RAW MATERIALS   **PRODUCTION**   **FINISHED GOODS**

MANUFACTURING

Figure 9.1. RFID Possible-State Vision

At this point, we reiterate that a company and its key business allies should prepare a customized version of the framework being discussed and use it to analyze how the various supply chain process steps can be improved through the use of RFID technology. The possibilities begin with raw materials and components needed for manufacture or production, where

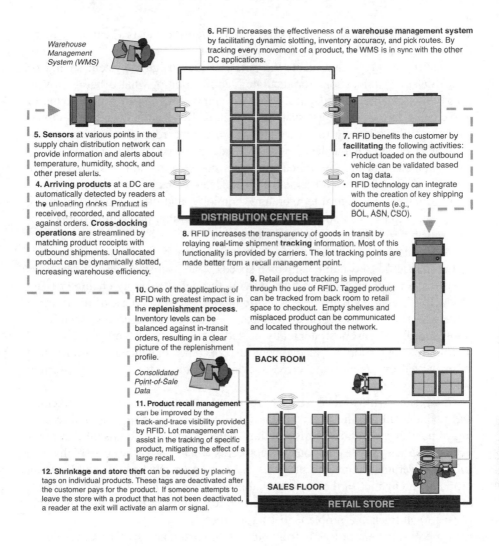

6. RFID increases the effectiveness of a **warehouse management system** by facilitating dynamic slotting, inventory accuracy, and pick routes. By tracking every movement of a product, the WMS is in sync with the other DC applications.

Warehouse Management System (WMS)

5. Sensors at various points in the supply chain distribution network can provide information and alerts about temperature, humidity, shock, and other preset alerts.

4. Arriving products at a DC are automatically detected by readers at the unloading docks. Product is received, recorded, and allocated against orders. **Cross-docking operations** are streamlined by matching product receipts with outbound shipments. Unallocated product can be dynamically slotted, increasing warehouse efficiency.

7. RFID benefits the customer by **facilitating** the following activities:
• Product loaded on the outbound vehicle can be validated based on tag data.
• RFID technology can integrate with the creation of key shipping documents (e.g., BOL, ASN, CSO).

DISTRIBUTION CENTER

8. RFID increases the transparency of goods in transit by relaying real-time shipment **tracking** information. Most of this functionality is provided by carriers. The lot tracking points are made better from a recall management point.

9. Retail product tracking is improved through the use of RFID. Tagged product can be tracked from back room to retail space to checkout. Empty shelves and misplaced product can be communicated and located throughout the network.

10. One of the applications of RFID with greatest impact is in the **replenishment process**. Inventory levels can be balanced against in-transit orders, resulting in a clear picture of the replenishment profile.

Consolidated Point-of-Sale Data

11. Product recall management can be improved by the track-and-trace visibility provided by RFID. Lot management can assist in the tracking of specific product, mitigating the effect of a large recall.

BACK ROOM

12. Shrinkage and store theft can be reduced by placing tags on individual products. These tags are deactivated after the customer pays for the product. If someone attempts to leave the store with a product that has not been deactivated, a reader at the exit will activate an alarm or signal.

SALES FLOOR

RETAIL STORE

Figure 9.1 (continued).

RFID can bring visibility to what is available to promise (what is in inventory), what is capable to promise (what inventory is in the system for manufacture), what is in transit (for possible delivery or diversion), and so forth. As indicated, tags can be integrated into the cartons or placed on individual items. Plans should be made so each carton and pallet will contain a tag with unique EPC numbers assigned when the tag is created or at an appropriate place within any later movement.

Readers of a type that meets the needs of the designed system should be placed in strategic locations for accurate identification of what is being moved; for receiving, picking, and packing actual shipments; and to report status of movements to the inventory system of record. Load authentication becomes streamlined by allowing truck weights to be compared with attributes of the contents reported on the tags. Security features serve to capture any illegal entries or movements. As indicated, errors are captured much earlier in the system, reducing the need for remediation and later reconciliation. Special sensors in the shipment can record temperature, humidity, and other conditions during transit and report fluctuations at the end of the journey, preventing damage or ensuring future loads are handled better.

Authentication of import products helps security by linking digital certification to specific EPC numbers, which speeds customs inspection and decreases the chances for counterfeit products moving through the supply chain. Arriving products are automatically detected throughout any warehouse or distribution center. Manual processing is eliminated, so costs are reduced and security is improved. With sensors strategically placed at the doors of the warehouse and distribution center, order management also becomes enhanced as information is integrated throughout any cross-docking operations for receiving, sorting, staging, and shipping.

Integration with warehouse management systems is facilitated for tracking and updating all inventory movement in real time with the reading and recording of each event within the distribution center. Validation to ensure that products, quantities, and destinations are correct is enhanced by the readers that can trigger a warning before the products are loaded on trucks or vans. Tracking products throughout further supply chain steps reduces loss and theft of inventory. In the event of incidents of tampering, lot control information is available to trace and track the problem to its source.

As any shipment proceeds from storage to customers, RFID readers detect all product movements in transit, at the store receiving door and inside the back room or retailing area, and can automatically report and prevent stock-out conditions. The readers on recycling bins can monitor tags and report when individual products have been placed on the retail shelves. Automatic inventory replenishment orders can be generated when needed, accelerated and made more accurate by supplementing the point-of-sale information with the RFID-gathered data. This consolidation step is a real advantage offered by the new technology. Finally, product recall management is simplified because tags allow monitoring of cases and pallets as they move backwards through the supply chain. All of these steps become even more enhanced when the RFID tagging is extended to individual items.

For companies looking to increase levels of control over what happens within a supply chain, RFID systems bring a new and higher degree of enhancement. By 2006–2007, we expect to see RFID tagging systems creating significant cost reductions, reducing working capital asset investments, eliminating much of the current theft and shrinkage, and introducing other operational improvements. One analyst predicts that by 2008–2009, "enterprises will tag more than 70 percent of their assets and generate operating-cost reductions of 1% to 3%. These reductions will be realized through reduction of lost assets, improved tracking of asset maintenance, and protection from theft, fraud, or injury" (Alvarez 2004).

British grocery retailer Tesco, moreover, has begun its investments in the future being described, without foisting the initial cost solely on suppliers — contrary to the conventional wisdom counseling that all cost will be borne by the upstream suppliers. This firm bought 4,000 RFID readers and 16,000 antennas for its U.K. stores and distribution centers through a contract with ADT Security Services. The equipment will be deployed with OatSystems, Inc.'s middleware and ADT's Device Commander, to synchronize data collection from the RFID devices. Readers will first be provided at dock and merchandising receiving doors for 1,300 Tesco Stores and 35 distribution centers to track cases and pallets of products. According to Gartner analyst Jeff Woods, "Tesco's decision to build up its infrastructure before bringing suppliers onboard will most likely lead to a more robust business case, because if they have to pay for their own tags, they're probably more rigorous with their assessment" (Sullivan 2005c, p. 35).

RFID CHALLENGE: COMPLIANCE TO VALUE

As a firm prepares its strategy and business roadmap, we should return to the original arguments for and against adoption of RFID technology. Using Figure 9.2 as a guide, dealing with the challenges moves across a spectrum — from meeting mandates and achieving compliance to creating values for all involved companies. This effort begins in the *basic adoption* area, by understanding the promises and skepticism surrounding RFID adoption. In this first step, the partners to an RFID deployment should directly confront the pertinent issues. A partnering diagnostic lab is advised to put the advocates and cynics in the same room and go through the pertinent issues. All arguments for or against adoption should be presented and settled, so an active and positive approach can be taken in the building of a strategy and action plan.

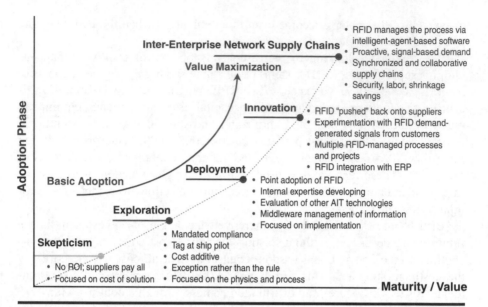

Figure 9.2. RFID Challenge: Compliance to Value

Beginning with the *skepticism* step, major arguments that there will be no return on investment (ROI) for some of the participants should be voiced. A subsequent discussion of the valid opportunities for improvement and actual possible results will either kill the project or move the focus to verifying the cost of a viable solution through an actual test. How benefits will be developed should be clearly identified, and an understanding of how savings will be shared should be outlined in this part of the process. It is at this phase that discussions should begin around what information will be generated by the RFID network, how and when that information will be shared, and most importantly, who will own the information.

In the absolutely necessary *exploration* step, the parties review how to cope with any mandated compliance issues by keeping costs and risk to a minimum. A tag-and-ship pilot is strongly recommended to bring an order-of-magnitude set of numbers to what the actual costs will be. Simulation techniques can be applied here to test various "what-if" scenarios and conditions of execution. Any added costs for the various constituents should be considered and a team formed to develop a first-pass cost/benefit estimate. Throughout what amounts to an intelligent evaluation phase, teams should work on exceptions rather than the rules. By definition, a tag-and-ship approach is an exception to established business processes. Goods that must be tagged either to meet a compliance requirement or as part of an exploratory pilot to examine the issues of RFID-based supply chain management will be segregated from the normal product flow and receive special handling. This step provides information to build out the "what-if" or future "could-be"-state vision — when all business processes are RFID enabled. While building these scenarios, it is critical to overlay the expected improvements in the underlying RFID technology as well as expected developments in RFID middleware. These assumptions will provide input for the firm's expected adoption and deployment plan.

As the partners enter the *deployment* step, focus goes to the specific points of adoption for RFID. At this step, information gathered from *skepticism* and *exploration* must be reviewed and filtered with new developments that have occurred over the time since the firm began its RFID initiatives. Both internal and external filters must be applied. Internal filters would primarily be new strategic directions for the firm and its partners. It is critical to understand and incorporate how new sourcing and distribution initiatives, new product introductions, new markets, etc. will affect the overall RFID deployment plans. As important as the internal filters are, projections of external filters such as tag cost, tag performance, RFID middleware functionality, projected customer mandates, and so forth have perhaps a greater weight when building the RFID deployment plan. Building an accurate set of projections for hardware costs, product availability, and integration costs as well as standards development will provide the input necessary when calculating ROI for various phases of the project and developing the overall business case. Developing strong relationships with RFID systems integrators and hardware and software providers is critical at this point in order to gather accurate and objective data.

With internal expertise developing, or augmented by external subject matter experts, an in-depth analysis can be made of the alternative automatic identification technologies that have application to the situations being considered. Middleware to manage the information will be one of the major considerations. Again, the focus should be kept on how the parties are going to implement whatever final plan is developed. As mentioned earlier, building an in-house RFID pilot lab will allow internal constituents (operations, manufacturing, distribution, packaging, etc.) and external trading partners to have a place to test and trial improved processes. As part of these efforts, an evolving process implementation and deployment plan should be appearing in the discussion.

For the sake of illustration, we have noted *innovation* as a separate and distinct phase in the process. Based on our experience, discussions of new RFID-enabled processes must be undertaken throughout each phase of adoption. In the *innovation* phase, the teams begin exercising their imagination by describing what an improved future state might look like and what benefits would accrue if all products were RFID tagged and communicated wirelessly via the

Internet to various control systems and software. This is the point where creative thinking wins out over critical thinking.

While the majority of the work produced during *innovation* will not provide "live" results (e.g., modifying a distribution center to handle only RFID-based transactions), the exercise of working through the potential benefits as part of a future state will present valuable input and direction to the firm's overall RFID blueprint. The time to critically think about results will come as the future-state vision is adjusted as part of the overall RFID blueprint and strategy. The team can then pick and choose the deployment path, based on the filters established as part of the overall strategy. For example, a food manufacturer might find that as part of its compliance to a customer's RFID mandate it has a fairly significant investment in fixed and handheld RFID readers. During the *innovation* phase, a possible scenario could be developed where this investment is leveraged into the receipt of raw materials (assuming its suppliers tagged product) to improve visibility of raw materials on hand, reduce or eliminate cycle counts, and improve product traceability as part of compliance to the bioterrorism legislation.

The team must push beyond the limitations of the technology and wrestle with the business case, as well as explore new business models. The team must cope with the issue that the cost of RFID will be incurred by the suppliers and eventually be pushed onto consumers. Through experimentation with what RFID demand generation signals from customers can do for supply chain efficiency, the participants will start to formulate potential paybacks from an effort. A prioritized list of the multiple RFID-managed processes and projects will flesh out exactly what can be enhanced, and the potential values for making the effort will become apparent.

Perhaps most importantly, a thorough understanding of the value of RFID-generated information must be documented and incorporated into both the business plan and emerging RFID strategy. Throughout this book, one of our key points is that the true value of RFID (as with any new technology introduced during the last 20 years, from PCs to e-mail, cell phones, Wi-Fi, etc.) is in the new benefits it will provide. Often the first argument thrown up against RFID implementation is "there is no ROI" or "it only benefits the retailers because they don't have to buy the tags." These arguments are narrowly focused and not well thought out. What is the ROI for e-mail? How did the finance department calculate the ROI on the first desktop PC purchase 20 years ago? The game will be won by those who understand and exploit new technologies to improve their current business and develop new business models. As part of the work during the *innovation* phase, the team must push out and explore all potential scenarios and look beyond the physical boundaries of RFID to identify new sources and uses of information.

As the players reach the *value maximization* area, and proceed into how to enhance *internetworked supply chains,* the diagnostic either will lead to a go-forward strategy and plan or the process will come to a screeching halt. Elements and learning from each preceding step must be incorporated into this phase, whether in terms of strategy development or actual implementation. At this point, there should be sufficient information and analysis to decide on the costs and benefits to be generated, which party will bear which costs, and how the information and risk will be shared across the network. How RFID will be deployed to manage the designated processes via intelligent-agent-based software will be on the table with defining metrics. How proactive, signal-based demand will be used to improve matching supply with demand will be understood. Mostly, how better synchronization and collaboration will create the best supply chains will be documented. All of the security issues will be explained and estimates made for cost savings, cost sharing, and benefit sharing throughout the extended enterprise.

The results of the diagnostic should lead to a defined and prioritized list of specific actions, to be taken by teams chartered by the participants. These teams will have a scope of what is to be accomplished, the resources necessary to complete the actions, a set of action steps with timetables for accomplishment, cost sharing and benefit sharing, and a means of establishing accurate costs and benefits from implementation. Where pilots are necessary (an advisable step), these will be scoped and defined and results verified.

Figure 9.3 helps guide the effort at this point. In the first step, a team will be assigned to define the physical elements of the agreed upon plan of action. Here the team identifies, reviews, and assesses the products targeted as part of the implementation plan and makes certain there is alignment around the physics of what will be happening. The team will also identify the extent of the RFID network being impacted by the deployment, including what class of tags will be used, what readers will be used, where they will be stationed, how they will communicate, and what facilities will be covered. A selection of the basic elements will be made (tags, readers, servers, and software suppliers). How, where, and what information will be collected, shared, filtered, and integrated with current enterprise resource planning (ERP), warehouse management systems, and other back office systems must also be identified. The means to install, pilot, test, maintain, support, and eventually bring the system online will complete this phase of the effort.

Another team should be dispatched to detail the process part of the plan. This team will review the proposed contracts to identify any areas of required compliance and how those matters will be satisfied. The team will select the target business process to be impacted and enhanced. A crucial step will be to

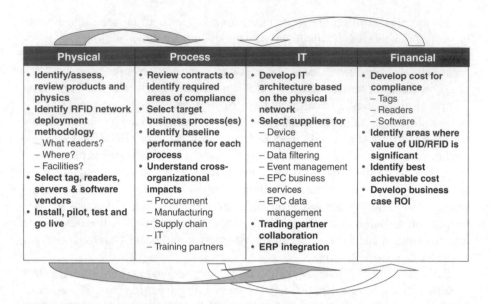

Physical	Process	IT	Financial

• **Identify/assess, review products and physics**
 • **Identify RFID network deployment methodology**
    What readers?
    – Where?
    – Facilities?
 • **Select tag, readers, servers & software vendors**
 • **Install, pilot, test and go live**
	• **Review contracts to identify required areas of compliance**
	 • **Select target business process(es)**
	 • **Identify baseline performance for each process**
	 • **Understand cross-organizational impacts**
	    – Procurement
	    – Manufacturing
	    – Supply chain
	    – IT
	    – Training partners
		• **Develop IT architecture based on the physical network**
		 • **Select suppliers for**
		    – Device management
		    – Data filtering
		    – Event management
		    – EPC business services
		    – EPC data management
		 • **Trading partner collaboration**
		 • **ERP integration**
			• **Develop cost for compliance**
			    – Tags
			    – Readers
			    – Software
			 • **Identify areas where value of UID/RFID is significant**
			 • **Identify best achievable cost**
			 • **Develop business case ROI**

Figure 9.3. Bringing Substantial Impact Across the Organization

establish baseline performance information for each process step affected, so proof of improvement will be clear and not debatable. This team will shoulder the responsibility for making certain the various stakeholders understand the cross-organizational impacts from deployment.

An information technology team will be chartered to develop the architecture based on the physical network outlined by the first team. This team will select the actual suppliers for device management, data filtering, event management, EPC business services, and EPC management. How the trading partners in the network will collaborate on purchase, installation, testing, and execution will be carefully explained. This team will, of course, clearly define how the system will be integrated with existing ERP systems.

A financial team will provide the defining metrics and cost/benefit analysis, including the cost to develop and deploy tags, readers and software. This team will identify areas where the value of unique identification and RFID will be significant. Through testing and pilots, the best achievable costs will appear and a business case containing a time frame with a reasonable ROI will be established. For a multiple-business-unit company, a series of such cases will be developed. In general for such multiunit organizations, the full scenario, from diagnostic through team recommendations and issuance of plans, should be performed.

The common thread throughout these efforts is the ability to answer the CEO's question: How will RFID improve my shareholders' value? If the preparation has been done thoroughly and correctly, answers can be provided for both strategic and tactical considerations. When ready for executive review and endorsement, these plans will cover how much investment will be made in time and resources, especially the commitments to costs for hardware, software, integration, and implementation. How much equipment the business units or operating divisions will need to purchase will be specified. That will include laser or chemical marking, tags, readers, software, middleware, and ERP module integration. Now the specific supply chain entities can find the intended leverage that will be created by the enhanced processing. What are the people going to do differently and how they will react to the huge amount of new data should be understood at this point.

Some supply chain expertise may be necessary to reach this point in an adoption cycle. Supply chain and RFID knowledge must be combined to lead an enterprise-wide deployment, combined with a reasonable strategy and business plan to harmonize what will at least be an initially resisted transformation. Throughout the analysis and start-up, expertise must be applied to document the actual costs and benefits, working from agreed upon baseline numbers. In particular, there is a need to understand the cost and functionality of an individual business unit's RFID implementation. Many firms begin with a single business unit and use the design criteria, amended for actual operating conditions, to build other implementations. As the effort expands, for example, there should be opportunities for cross-organizational purchasing synergies and even sharing of RFID infrastructure.

Along the way, a catalogue should be made of any significant savings generated from the deployment. Chase-Pitkin Home & Garden, a division of Wegmans Food Markets, has developed an action case in that respect. Chase-Pitkin "deployed predictive-analytics software from SPSS Inc. in order to stop the disappearance of $2.52 million to $3.24 million in merchandise, or 1.4% to 1.8% of its $180 million in annual revenue. A year and a half after its deployment, the application has reduced theft by more than $540,000." The application has been so successful that Chase-Pitkin will make the tool available to all departments and stores throughout 2005 (Sullivan 2005d, p. 67).

RESULTS CAN BE OUTSTANDING

Consistent with our thesis that the processing should be improved first, followed by technology enhancement, several firms are doing just that, as they use RFID to enhance necessary improvements to existing supply chain systems. An action story reported by *Supply Chain Management Review* illustrates the kind of success that can be achieved. Reporting on Gillette, an early adopter and strong advocate of RFID, the story indicated that this firm faced a series of supply chain dilemmas and came up with solutions that increased service levels by 10 percent, reduced inventories by 25 percent, and cut costs by 3 percent. The story begins in 2002, with Gillette, which sells not only its famous shaving products but Braun appliances, Duracell batteries, and Oral B dental products, facing low service levels. In its personal care line of products, the firm had results showing service levels as low as 80 percent achievement against a target of 98 percent — meaning as much as 20 percent of orders were not arriving when promised. With Gillette products in good demand, the company was not able to meet its customers' requirements.

Launching an internal improvement effort, dubbed "Functional Excellence," the firm embarked on a major effort to address its planning, manufacturing, order management, and deployment/delivery processes. Facing a typical inclination to add inventory to protect service, Gillette noted its inventories were among the highest in the industry. Obviously, something else had to work better. Functional Excellence had to cope with a "poor service, high inventory" situation. The first step was to benchmark the company against competitors to identify target areas for improvement. Areas needing attention included first ship fill rates, order fulfillment lead time, and expediting rush orders. To the company's dismay, it only ranked high in the last category, which of course required extra costs to meet customer needs.

The second step was to discuss the firm's current situation and improvement effort with key customers. These meetings and conversations had a sobering effect. They confirmed the seriousness of the problem and elaborated on the actual depth of the consequences, from the viewpoint of these buyers. End-to-end process mapping quickly followed, with an emphasis on pinpointing the areas needing improvement and finding suitable solutions. Multiple shipments were routinely needed to complete orders. Timing was not synchronized across planning, manufacturing, and delivery. Functional areas were using different definitions and measurements to determine quality of performance. Accountability for failure was very limited.

With the disturbing news under its belt, Gillette established 11 key levers as core elements in its turnaround program. Thousands of SKUs were eliminated, unnecessary order-to-delivery processes were curtailed, demand planning was overhauled, forecast accuracy was improved, and promotional efforts were enhanced. Concentrating on gaining manufacturing efficiency as well as higher service levels, Gillette began doing a better job of matching forecasts with demand volatility and manufacturing run frequency.

Throughout this process, the company had been planning to introduce RFID technology, after purchasing 500 million tags. Focusing on areas already covered in the book, the firm has been testing the technology in a variety of areas across its end-to-end processing. The result? All key performance indicators have moved in the right direction. Forecast accuracy has gone from less than 60 percent to 71 percent. Fill rates have reached 98 percent. Inventory is down 25 percent. A special benefit has been the increase in free cash flow. Overall, it is a great success story for one of the leading advocates for RFID, demonstrating clearly how RFID can enable improved processes in concert with other key business objectives.

CONCLUSIONS

Building a business case for RFID adoption and deployment will not be an easy task, in view of the strong opposition in many business sectors. The growing number of substantiating stories will serve to add impetus to acceptance, but our research indicates the battle is far from over. Far more validation is necessary, as well as more shrinking of the associated costs. In this chapter, we have presented the framework for building a solid case for RFID deployment. We now proceed to discuss how to set up the kind of tests and pilots that will minimize the risk of deployment and establish the real value for accepting this emerging technology and its applications.

10

CONSTRUCTING
A PRODUCTIVE
RFID PILOT

Amid all of the controversy surrounding RFID technology and its deployment, a significant number of businesses remain determined to move forward, often in the face of limited data and documented financial results. An equal or greater number are still not sure enough of the possible results and continue to wait for further developments. Still others remain opposed to adopting the technology. To validate the potential advantages to be gained from RFID deployment, a number of pilot projects are under way in a variety of industries, a technique we strongly endorse.

From tests by automotive firms and brewers to consumer products, health care, logistics providers, manufacturers, and retailers, companies are attempting to come to grips with the promises and problems and to integrate RFID into a comprehensive supply chain strategy and business plan. Global consortiums of universities, interested companies, and dedicated organizations have been developing all sorts of infrastructures using RFID tags and Auto-ID systems. What these pilot efforts are proving is that using radio waves to track products and provide visibility and real-time access to status and location presents another means to make supply chains more effective and satisfying.

Typical of the conditions we have been describing, the investigations into how to apply the technology meet with differing opinions. Jonathan Byrnes, writing for the *Harvard Business School Working Knowledge* publication, positions the cynics' argument. "In the system envisioned by some consortium leaders," he states, "literally everything would be tagged with chips that 'announce' identity when hit with a non-line-of-sight electromagnetic field. This system would have a common identification convention and set of standards. In theory, a store, warehouse, or factory with Auto-ID could be hit with an electromagnetic pulse, and the contents would be instantly known. To some, this view seemed sufficiently far-fetched that they wrote off the whole concept, and to others it raised serious privacy concerns" (Byrnes 2003).

In spite of the opinions and concerns mentioned by Byrnes and others, the tests and pilots continue to appear, bringing documentation to the possible supply chain enhancements and return on investment. So, how can a firm decide on its course of action? While many firms remain frozen in place, wary of the costs and risks, we see the only way to verify what can or cannot happen being accomplished through a carefully designed and controlled experiment that identifies actual operating conditions and documents the costs and benefits. In this chapter, we continue to consider the pros and cons confronting RFID deployment, as we indicate how a pilot test can be arranged and conducted to prove or disprove the validity of applying RFID as an enhancement to supply chain processing, for a particular firm in a particular industry.

THE RANGE OF TESTING IS EXTENSIVE

Asset management pilots are one type of business exercise being used to determine what can be accomplished with RFID as a means of reducing asset needs, eliminating inventory losses, and helping to reduce shrinkage. Existing pilots include tracking heavy rolls of paper that can lose their bar code information when stored under conditions of high humidity. Another covers "heating, ventilating, and air-conditioning dampers that are installed with bar codes facing a concrete structure, rendering them unreadable or unreachable for maintenance tracking" (Alvarez 2004).

Still more pilots are under way to determine the value in tracking livestock; contents of a ship's cargo, railroad box cars, and ore cars; and products moving in and delivered by trucks. Still other tests are being used to determine the viability of the technology to assist with airline baggage handling, to prevent automobile theft, to deal with illegal entries into a country or manufacturing site, and to improve maintenance of important operating equipment. FedEx is testing RFID wristbands, for example, that can be used instead of keys to unlock doors on delivery trucks. That company estimates the loss of keys by drivers costs an average of $200 or more per incident.

The ongoing investigations, moreover, are not limited to huge corporations or giant retailers. The DeKalb County Juvenile Court system offers an example of just how far investigation into potential advantages can go. An estimate of the number of hours spent looking for lost files needed by judges in this system reaches ten hours per week. Using RFID as an enabler, a search was conducted to eliminate the causes of misplaced or lost files to ensure judges would have the data needed to make quicker decisions. The court system used $50,000 from the Georgia court's annual budget "to install an RFID system from 3M," says Dale Phillips, director of court services. "The 3M RFID tracking system would save at least $30,000 a year in productivity gains" (Sullivan 2005f, p. 44).

The U.S. Department of Homeland Security (DHS) is experimenting with RFID to track foreigners entering and leaving the United States. That agency is trying to find the means for establishing tighter security, without adding to the inconvenience of normal travelers. RFID tags were being tested at a simulated port operation in spring 2005 and at border crossings in Arizona, New York, and Washington states from July through spring 2006. These tests will help DHS determine whether to affix RFID tags to passports, visas, or other documents visitors are required to carry during their visits to the United States. To protect privacy, the tags "won't hold visitors' personal information only serial codes linked to information stored in the [DHS]'s US-visitor data base. The codes will be meaningless to any third party trying to access the information" (Chabrow 2005b, p. 26).

THREE LEVELS OF PILOTS

To validate the use of RFID technology, three types of pilots are outlined below. Regardless of which type of pilot approach is chosen, however, there are several fundamental themes which flow throughout all successful experiments. Ensuring that these themes, or pilot objectives, are being addressed and managed as part of a firm's pilot work will help to achieve a successful pilot:

1. **Strong project manager** — Put someone in charge with good project management skills, training in RFID technology, and at a senior enough level in the organization to marshal the necessary resources and support. The project manager should expect to be assigned full time during the course of the project.

2. **Cross-functional support team** — It is critical to have the involvement and support of a well-staffed cross-functional project team. Team member representation should be from IT, supply chain, operations, manufacturing, marketing, packaging, finance, loss prevention, and distribution. Team members should expect to spend from 25 to 50 percent of their time during the course of the project.

3. **Short timeline duration** — RFID pilots should be broken up into milestones that take no longer than three months to complete. This requirement is necessary in order to quickly assess progress, adjust the overall strategy, and test new or alternative scenarios. This will take a fair amount of planning and coordination on the part of the project manager.

4. **Senior-level executive support** — Align with an executive sponsor with strong organizational influence, to help the project team negotiate through the various organizational challenges that will be faced. This sponsor must be able to see and communicate strategic issues that the company will be addressing through the use of RFID.

5. **Clear project goals and communication** — The team must provide updates on objectives, milestones, next steps, and lessons learned throughout the duration of the project. These updates can be sent via e-mail, posted on the company's intranet, or given during scheduled staff meetings.

Using the framework of adoption discussed in the previous chapter, Computer Sciences Corporation, a leading developer of pilot options to assist companies in understanding the advantages, disadvantages, problems, and pitfalls with RFID applications, recommends three levels of pilot tests and operations: compliance only, compliance with internal benefits, and joint venture pilots. Due to the broad scope of RFID and since the focus of this book is the application of RFID to improve supply chain operations, we will limit our discussion to supply chain applications of RFID whether for internal operational improvements or to meet customer requirements. The three pilots are described as follows:

■ **Compliance only** — Tag at shipping (also known as "slap and ship") and provide data in the defined Electronic Product Code (EPC) form. This approach involves limited risk and effort, but has no internal benefit. This is an exception-based process: tagging only those goods shipped to specific customers based on RFID mandates. Although this type of implementation returns no financial benefit to the company, it does limit financial and technology risk, as well as serve to demonstrate the firm's ability, or lack thereof, to be compliant with a critically important customer. It also provides the foundation of needed learning for future use and application of RFID technology under conditions that will benefit the company. Implementation can be relatively simple and inexpensive (less than $150,000) and accomplished quickly when working with one vendor.

■ **Compliance with internal benefit** — This approach involves a broader examination of all supply chain operations and performance to seek out any and all areas for RFID-enabled improvements. Typically, the outcome of this approach is to tag earlier within internal operations to provide benefit from improved product information, provided by improved raw material and finished goods visibility. Compliance is the launching point, and this option provides the ability to demonstrate how a company can leverage the technology to achieve internal benefits as well as critical compliance. A detailed RFID blueprint and RFID strategy must be developed to outline how the phases of RFID deployment should occur. Coordination between anticipated customer mandates, generation of internal benefits, and projection of external developments (e.g., tag cost projections) must be developed and used as base assumptions when developing the RFID strategy.

The pilot will require more complex systems modifications and working out the necessary interfaces. Depending on the degree of needed integration, RFID middleware may be needed as a separate system or existing systems may have a bolt-on RFID application to manage the data generated by RFID. The pilot will also show the required changes to existing internal processes to reap the greatest improvement from any serious effort. Typically, this approach requires an initial "proof-of-concept" to test the hypothesis developed in a very limited scope so as to manage risk. Lessons learned from the proof-of-concept are then incorporated into a revised pilot plan than may encompass several phased pilots. Due to the more extensive nature of implementation and integration (in terms of quantity of product tagged, reader infrastructure, systems integration, etc.), these pilots require longer planning and design phases.

■ **Joint venture pilot** — Tag at a supplier and track product from suppliers through manufacturing process to customer delivery. This is the most complex but often most fruitful pilot and will illustrate more of the issues surrounding development of the RFID technology. A joint venture effort demands application of mutual resources and assets and generally leads to the development of larger business benefits. By its nature, multiple parties must commit resources to the effort and share in the risks and costs. Although these types of pilots are rare at this point in the history of RFID adoption, we believe that more companies will undertake this type of approach in order to share benefits, risks, and information in a collaborative fashion. Through our own work, we have seen a version of this type of pilot in large multidivisional corporations (many of which are global defense suppliers). In these situations, there is awareness that solutions, vendor relations, and strategies are developed independently, without coordination across business units, posing a greater risk and higher expense. A coordinated, corporate-led RFID project team composed of members from the various business units can leverage knowledge, experience, and expenses across the business during these pilots. Additionally, we believe that industry trade associations (such as the Grocery Manufacturers Association, National Association of Manufacturers, and others) are in a unique position to champion, develop, and support industry solutions targeted to the needs of their constituents.

CONSTRUCTING THE PILOT

The first step in creating any pilot is to have a reason, one that is explained in clear business-based language. As shown in Figure 10.1, at the very least there should be an RFID-related revenue opportunity, either through sustaining existing business or generating new sales. An RFID implementation can run from about $300,000 to several million, depending on the size and existing technical infrastructure of the companies involved in the project. We have already referenced the one operation set up by Procter & Gamble in Spain for less than $100,000. It can include upgrades to a warehouse management system that

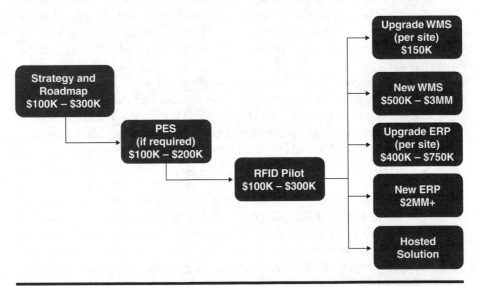

Figure 10.1. RFID Revenue Opportunities: RFID Implementations Can Run from $300,000 to Several Million Dollars, Depending on the Size, Need, and Existing Technological Infrastructure of the Companies Involved

could run $150,000 per site. For a completely new warehouse management system, the costs could rise to $500,000 to $3 million. Where an upgrade to an enterprise resource planning (ERP) system is required, the cost will generally fall between $400,000 to $750,000. Where a new ERP system is needed, the costs could reach $2 million. Hosted solutions by qualified third-party providers will depend on the job specifications, but will be at the upper end of the spectrum. These cost estimates do not include the ongoing costs of tag supplies, maintenance, and support. To cover these initial costs, a firm must have some sort of revenue flow at risk or be capable of improving a critical part of the supply chain processing to justify the necessary investment.

Beginning with the *compliance-only pilot*, described in Figure 10.2, the firm selects products or categories of products that are RFID mandated by a large customer. If constructed correctly, to minimize cost and risk, these pilots generally focus on low-volume, high-priced items with in-transit visibility benefits. Selecting environmental and product characteristics that perform best with current off-the-shelf RFID technology is also advisable. It has been our experience over the past several years that no one tag performs best across all types of product packaging and that certain manufacturers are developing niche expertise with particular tags for use on different materials. For example, we have always selected tags manufactured by Avery Dennison for their performance on difficult products such as water and metal. This conclusion is further supported by the recent testing results published by the RFID Alliance Lab (copies of which may be purchased from rfidjournal.com).

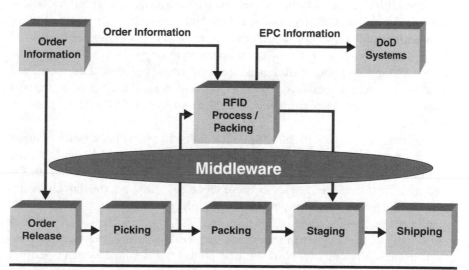

Figure 10.2. Compliance-Only Pilot

Several vendors should be selected for tag performance evaluation, and this can be performed either internally or through contracting with many of the RFID testing labs that are beginning to appear. Read performance tests will support the appropriate selection of tags, as well as determine the optimum placement of the tag on the case and pallet configuration. This information is then used to begin the construction of appropriate read point portals. These portals can be placed at the dock door, packing lines, and palletizing areas. Portals consist of a reader and at least one antenna oriented to capture the highest number of reads. Physical, on-site, testing is required to determine the optimal location and configuration of the portal. The selection of the tag normally will drive which RFID label printer to purchase to support this limited installation. Software to assign the EPC and number and capture and associate the information with current product files must also be purchased, installed, and integrated, based on project requirements.

As this approach is an exception-based process, the procedure typically begins by taking products in the designated categories out of the normal pack-and-ship processing. Depending on the current manufacturing and distribution processes, this may involve a degree of repacking in order to tag each case and then apply a new pallet tag and label. Tag reads will have to be performed at the case and pallet level to ensure that the product shipped meets the customer requirements. This step also provides a degree of quality assurance in the event the customer starts noting a decrease in reads upon receipt. The supplier will have documentation that good reads were received when shipped.

The standard transaction data should be sent to the appropriate parties and the information kept available for customer maintenance and forms to be determined during the pilot. An estimated budget should be prepared and compared with actual costs after the pilot is completed. Costs should be estimated on a per-shipment-point basis, with an approximation of the one-time cost for the initial solution. Labor will depend on local rates, but should be calculated for about 30 seconds per box. The tag cost will depend on actual purchased agreements, but will vary from about $0.21 to $0.45 per RFID label based on types and volumes.

The scenario changes slightly for a pilot involving *compliance with internal benefit*, illustrated in Figure 10.3. It has been our approach to begin this type of pilot with an assessment of current supply chain operations and an understanding of performance metrics of these processes. Next we overlay an explanation of the future vision of new or revised processes enabled through RFID, essentially the *innovation* activities discussed in Chapter 9. This step provides a gap analysis and begins the roadmap for RFID piloting, deployment, and business case development. Now the first point of application is dependent on

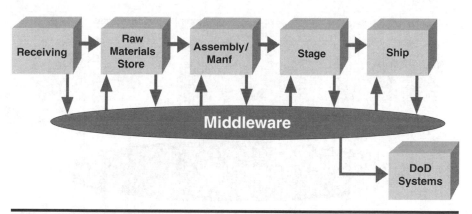

Figure 10.3. Compliance with Internal Benefit Pilot

identification of the business value, that is, determining what the company is trying to fix or improve. The product selection criteria focus more on items with high operational costs as a result of stock rotation issues, problems with shrink or theft, critical shortages in supply at the point of need, or lack of visibility in the current supply chain processing. Items that potentially cross multiple company divisions or business units or items that are sent out for subassembly, repackaging, or sterilization become candidates.

The process involves tagging products within the company's normal procedures. The idea is to leverage RFID and the improved visibility it provides to create benefits to current operations. Solutions should also have a direct bearing on meeting key customer compliance requirements. In fact, many of the first activities in terms of tag selection and portal construction are identical to the compliance-only approach. The pilot should demonstrate both the RFID technology issues as well as the ability to establish internal benefits from the improved visibility. Costs for the budget are estimated on a single product per solution basis, with an approximation of the one-time cost for the initial solution. Labor is again estimated based on local conditions, but should be expected to turn into a net savings. The tag cost will vary between $0.21 and $0.45.

For a *joint venture* pilot (our most favored test), outlined in Figure 10.4 for a hypothetical supplier to the U.S. Department of Defense (DOD), the first point of application is dependent on identification of business values across a supply chain network. Here the product selection criteria should be a collaborative effort and cover items that require significant operational effort based on current lack of exchanged data. Critical components for military compliance, for example, should be brought into the discussion, so questions around

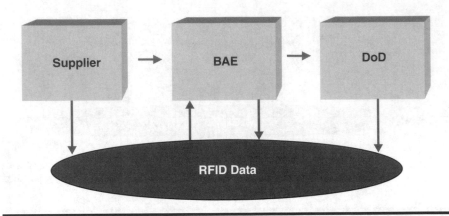

Figure 10.4. Joint Venture Pilot

life cycles, software upgrades, expiration dates, and short supply are answered. This discussion should also include how the exchange of unique identification (UID) data will be accomplished and what benefits will accrue from sharing this information on a real-time basis. Also, the scope of the solution should be broadened to allow for active RFID technology that can be applied on reusable plastic containers that might move in a closed loop between supplier and customer.

The process starts with tags being applied at the supplier level that will benefit supplier and buyer, with improved visibility of raw materials as well as receipt operations. Throughout this test, efforts should be made to determine how to use RFID for internal improvement opportunities for both parties. In the military case, providing compliance to DOD can be combined with eliciting some form of life cycle management test to demonstrate the improved real-time visibility to asset deployment versus having extra safety stocks. We also believe that due to the typically high value of certain military assets, there is a signifi-cant opportunity to use remote sensor-based networks that would not only monitor inventory levels but also monitor environmental and security condi-tions. Costs for the budget are estimated on a single product and solution basis and the approximate one-time cost for the initial solution. Here the cost is extremely dependent on the extent of the supply chain being tracked and the number of reader location requirements. For companies that are complying with the DOD's UID/RFID mandate, accurately capturing the expenses involved in compliance is critical, as there is the opportunity to include these costs as part of the normal administrative overhead calculation allowed as part of govern-ment contracts.

KEYS TO DEPLOYING RFID SUCCESSFULLY

There are a number of important factors in conducting a successful RFID pilot. First, the participants should find a source for practical and impartial advice on Auto-ID, automatic identification technology (AIT), and RFID technology. With this help, the appropriate people to be involved in the pilot should be educated and aligned around their mutual understanding of the RFID technology and how it can be used to develop and leverage network communications within the firm's unique supply chain environment. The hardware to be used, the supporting software, and the potential suppliers of the components should be discussed and evaluated and facts sorted from fiction, so careful selections are made. The pilot will prove or disprove the validity of the effort, but poor up-front selection can kill a well-intentioned test.

The parties involved should establish a business process, complete with process map, describing what is targeted for improvement, so a focused strategy can be evolved after the pilot. Of critical importance is the need to develop a return on investment analysis to support whatever business plan is created. The focus should be on the fundamental impacts from EPC and RFID, established through a careful evaluation of the issues, problems, and opportunities to be dealt with by integrating AIT and RFID data into existing ERP systems. Identifying where to start should not be a trivial matter, but rather the subject of serious discussion — to gain alignment around which business processes can benefit the most by becoming RFID enabled (with minimal risk). A checklist is also beneficial and should include:

- Create a sound tactical plan, which can be modified as the test evolves.
- Understand the physics of the planned system and the appropriate use of the technology.
- Have enough knowledge of the physics and technology to easily sort through the myth and hype circling around RFID.
- Have an appreciation of how RFID complements other Auto-ID technologies as well as what new technologies are on the horizon.
- Have a business purpose for the pilot with baseline conditions and revenue, cost, and benefit impacts. Be prepared and able to articulate this purpose in terms of strategic direction and tactical issues.
- Select the most appropriate products and categories for the initial test, so results have pertinence across the organization.
- Conduct a negotiation process with suppliers in an environment of having a desire for understanding and appreciation before committing significant capital and resources to an RFID effort.

- Identify those within the firm most capable of participating in a complex and possibly extended evaluation process.
- Prepare a preliminary budget to cover expected costs and carefully document each step in the pilot.
- Evaluate the firm's infrastructure to determine where new responsibilities must be created and where shifts in responsibilities might occur.
- Evaluate the firm's system architecture in terms of whether it is capable of handling the larger data loads that will be created by RFID.
- Evaluate whether the firm's current suppliers of Auto-ID technology (bar code and other system automation technologies) can support the RFID initiatives.
- Establish a plan for introducing the technology or not, based on the results of the pilot tests (i.e., have criteria for making a go or no-go decision).
- Compare results against the growing number of pilots being conducted by competitors and those in other industries.
- Prepare the organization for further test and initial implementations.
- Be prepared to answer the CEO's question: "How will RFID improve my shareholders' value?"

OTHER ISSUES FOR CONSIDERATION

Entering the RFID world can be accompanied by much apprehension, as there are still many unanswered questions and concerns. For those willing to go forward, our best advice is to approach the first test or pilot as an effort to accept a new and innovative technology, much as was done when entering the worlds of computers and wireless telecommunication. Consider the effort as something that is not about the details of the emerging technology, but about accepting a vision or a projection of what can be an improved future state of processing. Entering the RFID arena is about being part of those who are early to recognize the advantages offered and those who want to grasp an understanding of how the technology will improve specific processes and the necessary flows of information. Through the experimenting and testing that will occur during the pilot, participants will gain the knowledge needed to exploit this exciting new innovation.

Understand further that RFID technology is an enabler and the foundation for gaining visibility and information about what is occurring across an end-to-end supply chain in real time. Approach the pilot as a means of finding out where there are major gaps in supply chain processing and weaknesses such as shrinkage and excess inventories. The technology then becomes the means to reduce or eliminate those gaps and bring remedies to the weaknesses. As the pilot evolves, be certain to identify all of the opportunities that can be affected by RFID, taking time to answer the following questions:

- What are the business objectives we are trying to accomplish?
- What further information and knowledge will better enable us to reach these objectives?
- What are the risks associated with our effort?
- Which processes can be enhanced and by how much?
- Which supply chain partners are critical to a successful effort? How do we gain their collaboration?
- What final values do we want to see from a successful pilot?

Added to these questions should be a list of deliverables for the pilot, accomplishments that will make the effort a success in the eyes of the most critical cynics. Serving customers faster, reducing shrinkage, increasing security, not being out of stock, stimulating new product introductions, capturing new business, assisting manufacturing efficiencies, better organizing inventory, and making better deliveries should be on the list. In addition, attention should be paid to developing differentiating factors for the supply chain network, which will distinguish it in the eyes of the most coveted customers.

Finally, we advise following the lessons learned from previous tests and pilots. Begin and end the pilot with a determination to settle the values that can be gained from introducing RFID technology to your supply chain. Put the early emphasis on process improvement and information transfer rather than the technology. Challenge existing assumptions, beliefs, and culture, as they invariably stand in the way of progress. Make the people observing the test think in terms of what is possible as well as evaluating the impediments. It has been our experience that this is an organic process. Many of the best uses of RFID came from small, unrelated pilots after others in the organization understood the capability of RFID. Partner carefully with the suppliers of the elements of the infrastructure to make certain the system selected meets the needs of the intended applications. Above all, aim the pilot at putting to bed the controversy existing across your organization.

SUMMARY

The best way to separate the hype from the reality surrounding the adoption and deployment of RFID technology is to set up and execute a controlled experiment or pilot, through which the values can be verified or obviated. In this chapter, we have outlined a technique that has been very useful for our purposes in helping clients validate the potential improvements that can be made to a supply chain. Three approaches can be taken, depending on the intended scope and the degree of risk you are willing to assume. With the results of a carefully planned pilot, a firm will be able to satisfy the cynics and the advocates with documented results and improvements to key metrics, with enough gain to create the necessary return on investment.

11

NEXT STEPS

In spite of the current resistance to acceptance and deployment of RFID technology, difficulties will be overcome as costs are lowered, usage extended, and benefits documented. Participating businesses will find enough added values to generate reasonable returns on investments, and their successes will inspire further deployment. As adoption takes hold and the number of factual documentations increases, it will become more apparent that RFID technology is not just a means of complying with heavy-handed mandates from a few very large purchasing organizations. It will become an enabler within supply chains, creating the necessary visibility to introduce a host of improvements — to efficiency, safety, security, counterfeiting, theft, shrinkage, shortages, inventory management, and more.

The technology will also spread into other areas of usage, broadcasting its usefulness and potential application. The April 15, 2005 issue of *USA Today* offered such an example. The newspaper noted, "When 20,000 runners take to the streets of Hopkinton, Mass., for the start of Monday's 109th Boston Marathon, race officials can track their progress electronically. Transponders, laced into a shoe of each entrant, will keep tabs on the runners." How do they work? The 3/16-inch, 0.2-ounce ChampionChip is a timing device. Every runner loops it into their laces through holes in the chip, fitting the chip snugly inside their instep. The chip identifies each runner's bib number and records when the runner crosses the start line, regardless of when the starting gun is fired. There are 11 checkpoints that record runners as they pass. When a runner passes a checkpoint, a mat picks up the runner's time and chip code. Data from the mat are downloaded into a laptop computer and sent to a database near the finish line. According to the article, "the information is also posted on www.bostonmarathon.org."

Proponents will discover that as computing power and data storage capabilities have increased and time for communication decreased, the challenge becomes data reasoning — determining the value of the enormous amount of business knowledge now at our disposal. We live in a state where there is more than enough knowledge to make an intelligent decision, but an insufficient amount of intelligent analysis to make the right decisions at the appropriate time. It is a time to use technology as an aid to interpreting what the data are revealing without undue delay in making appropriate responses. RFID will be a key ingredient to making the most of that interpretation as it brings instant access to information and knowledge about movements throughout supply chains of virtually any description. A further advantage will appear with the use of avatars, or intelligent software-based agents, that make decisions about rerouting shipments and changing inventory movements to meet actual needs.

It will also be discovered that RFID can play an important role in the ubiquitous movement toward a wireless business environment, wherein companies take advantage of mobile equipment to keep tabs on global supply chains and exchange information rapidly in real-time formats, commonly called edge computing or managing the edge of the enterprise. In this environment, wireless communication will prevail because it allows so much flexibility in terms of location, from the point of data access to the movements throughout a supply chain network. Important information will be put in the hands of those who need the knowledge — sales personnel, truck drivers, receivers, sorters, packers, and so forth.

Wireless systems will fill the gap between fixed structures like offices that contain all of the necessary back room information and the ever-increasing number of mobile workers. As businesses come to realize the importance of optimization across extended enterprises, ever-greater opportunities will arise for real-time access and collaboration between what can often be global constituents. A 225-year-old marine terminal operator found just such an opportunity when SSA Marine tested a new cargo container tracking system to more accurately track containers moving through its California ports. Under the old system, workers would log each container's identification number, "often stacked five high and six lanes wide throughout hundreds of acres of land." According to Ed DeNike, chief operating officer of SSA terminals, "10% to 20% of the container IDs aren't copied correctly, which causes the company to lose track of containers" (Hulme 2005b).

SSA began testing a system provided by WhereNet Corporation, which uses RFID tags on container-handling equipment like cranes to track specific locations. "An optical character-recognition system installed on the cranes captures an identification number from the side of a cargo container. That ID number and the location of the cargo-handling equipment are wirelessly transmitted to business-intelligence applications, which pinpoint the location and status of each container." DeNike says the solution should help track cargo containers while reducing the errors from lost containers (Hulme 2005b).

RFID will be at the center of efforts aimed at improving health care provision and facilitating some of life's simple processes. Some companies are already far down the road with their intentions. Science Applications International Corporation is developing technology for the U.S. Department of Defense and Department of Homeland Security which will use wireless sensors full of computer power to help "secure U.S. borders, bridges, power plants, and ships by detecting suspicious movements or dangerous cargo and radioing warnings back to a command center" (Ricadela 2005, p. 33).

British Petroleum plc, the large oil company, has an effort under way to reduce the cost of monitoring equipment at its Cherry Point, Washington oil refinery, from thousands of dollars per measurement to hundreds. The company's objective is to replace large wired sensors with wireless ones in its business network. Hewlett-Packard has tests under way as well, with wireless networked sensors at a warehouse in Memphis, Tennessee, as part of its plan to redesign how companies can manage the flow of goods. "A prototype wireless network of small video-camera sensors hooked to image-recognition software works in concert with radio-frequency identification technology to make sure inventory is put in the right place. The cameras track goods as they move through the warehouse, and those images get matched with RFID tag numbers that describe them" (Ricadela 2005, p. 33).

In this concluding chapter, we take a look at the road to the future, as we consider the next steps a company should consider before or after a commitment has been made to adopt RFID technology into supply chain processing. We also will look into the future to see what emerging technologies may have an impact on RFID deployments, as well as what new technologies are around the corner. Our purpose is to once again set aside the conflict and resistance to what we see as an inevitable technology trend and explain how wireless communications are also a part of businesses of the future. The combination of using RFID to establish greater visibility into what is happening inside a supply chain and to enhance the use of wireless technology represents two movements that can no longer be ignored.

BETTER DATA IS THE CENTRAL ISSUE

There is, of course, the need for development of better data standards to allow the kind of far-reaching improvements in our future-state vision, but there are enough efforts under way and bearing fruit that we see this problem resolved in the next two to three years. The real-time exchange of useful data regardless of platform or application is on the horizon, and we will witness overcoming rigid company-centric enterprise resource planning systems so knowledge can be more easily shared across business networks.

Eventual placement of RFID as a tool in a system with full visibility into the end-to-end supply chain processing is within our grasp. Depending on which analyst reports you read, the market for RFID hardware, software, and services is expected to grow at a compound annual rate of 10 to 28 percent per year over the next five to seven years. As the market for RFID technology and services continues to expand, we expect that costs will continue to decline and that the core technologies will become standard and commoditized. With actual cost and benefits better defined, the learning curves will lead to more distinct roadmaps by industry and application. The emphasis will shift from the current focus on the physics of RFID to the data-rich capabilities of RFID-enabled processes. The end result will be an abundance of data not now available to improve virtually every step in supply chain processing.

Under these new conditions, data becomes the key for leveraging an infrastructure and enhancing current performance. Through what will no doubt be a series of incremental implementations across a multitude of companies, successful architectures will arise and include:

- Cross-division collaborative opportunities to leverage the greater scale of a full business
- Data capture more quickly from sources previously excluded from supply chain analysis
- Insights into how to improve process steps and final delivery from a supply chain to end consumers
- Understanding on how to integrate reams of information into sensible business decisions

As we have consistently argued, RFID plays well in this scenario, but as just one tool, allowing buyers and sellers as well as shippers and receivers to see what is going on inside their enterprises. Visibility becomes the new ante in this environment, leading to increased sales, shorter cycle times, better service, and availability of products at the time of need, along with inventory reductions. RFID becomes the key tool to apply data in unlocking some of the mysteries in business processing. The result is a superior intelligent value network, with differentiating characteristics in the eyes of the customers.

This data generation and its value for users require considerable effort, however. Such conditions will only be reached through collaboration across a wide range of fragmented constituents. Applications must be carefully structured and used to guide implementations, while maintaining the proper balance between the physics, process, business cases, and data opportunity. Data management is crucial in this environment — to control and make practical use of what is expected to be an avalanche of new information. Hardware and readers need to be tactically deployed for best benefits, and the tags need to be selected and attached to the goods moving through the supply chain at the point at which greatest value can be achieved. All of the companies pictured, and more, will be involved in structuring the many systems that will continue to appear and validate the premises we have espoused.

With this clarification, adoption will be made easier and cross many industry boundaries. As progress is made, the concepts will be proven and more firms will follow. As RFID becomes more accepted, so will the complementary technologies at work in the contemporary business scene. Among those will be wireless technology.

RFID IN A WIRELESS ENVIRONMENT

Wireless sensor network technology is just one of several technologies that could turn into the next large technology-inspired market. While progress is mostly in the hands of military-funded academic research and some developmental organizations, supply-chain-oriented businesses are watching closely to see where the effort is headed. We see systems becoming linked together with sensors to detect changes in temperature, pressure, moisture, soil conditions, light, sound, or electromagnetism, with RFID reporting on the findings. Most importantly, we now have the tools and software to act on sensor data remotely (on the edge of the enterprise) and manage transactions at the item level. As the cost of tags continues to fall, the combination with sensing technology will only increase.

One possible breakthrough could be "mesh networking" software that "lets each device wake up for a fraction of a second when it has an interesting result to transmit, and then relay that information a few yards to its nearest neighbor. Instead of every sensor transmitting its information to a remote base station, an electronic bucket brigade moves data until it reaches a central computer where it can be stored and analyzed" (Ricadela 2005, p. 34). Our description of RFID throughout this book has focused on the tag-to-reader transaction; mesh networking is all about a tag-to-tag transaction — things communicating with each other.

This type of communication architecture is especially useful in situations where the antenna/reader infrastructure is too far away from all tags, such as large warehouses, outdoor storage depots, or battlefields. While certainly more expensive than the low-cost EPC standard passive tags we have focused on, there are many high-value asset applications where mesh networking can take hold at the item or asset level of tracking. Boeing, Chevron-Texaco, Honeywell, Motorola, and Siemens are busy exploring this facet of the technology scenario.

As the mobile workforce continues to expand in size and sophistication, bearing cell phones, personal digital assistants, and RIM BlackBerries in their pockets and the new generation of laptops in their valises, communication moves instantly from central offices to any spot around the world. That is the future we envision, replete with tiny chips and sensors and RFID readers and antennas to transmit more and more knowledge of the surrounding environment. The new wireless capabilities will eventually be harmonized with existing systems, allowing choices for expediting the transfer of knowledge so critical to advanced supply chain management techniques. Opportunities to extract business value, through the use of wireless technology in supply chains, have never been greater. Beginning with processes that are currently mobile in nature, and progressing to those that are inhibited, new approaches can be developed to expand access and speed data transfer.

When a pharmacy orders a controlled substance, for example, from a distributor, or when the distributor orders similar products from a manufacturer, a mandated paper trail ensues. The U.S. Drug Enforcement Administration (DEA) and the pharmaceutical industry are close to issuing modifications to the regulations which will allow the replacement of paper-based forms with electronic transactions featuring digital certificates. The Controlled Substance Ordering System, developed by PEC Solutions, Inc., will require technology investments across the industry, but will "put an end to a time-consuming and expensive process using the DEA's Form 222, which is meant to prevent certain pharmaceutical drugs from being used illegally and to ensure a sufficient supply for legitimate uses" (McGee 2005, p. 26).

At the National Retail Federation's annual conference in New York City in January 2005, Metro Group AG presented an RFID-enabled hanging garment sorter that the company claims can automate the routing of 4,000 to 8,000 garments every hour, compared to 150 pieces using manual sorting. "The RFID application is just one of several the German retailer has under way at an RFID Innovation Center it opened in July 2004 in Neuss-Norf, Germany." Marks & Spencer is enlarging its RFID efforts by tagging 3.5 million food and produce delivery trays. It takes about "10 seconds to read a stack of RFID-tagged produce trays, compared with between 30 and 40 seconds for bar-coded trays, according to the U.K. retailer" (Sullivan 2005g, p. 30).

Consider an everyday situation that comes under the microscope of what we are discussing. Picture a walk through a hospital or health care facility where an elderly patient is sleeping quietly in bed under multiple blankets. A doctor pauses on her rounds and clicks on her wireless tablet personal computer, which is equipped with an RFID reader. The device sends a signal to an RFID tag embedded in the patient's identification bracelet, hidden by the bedding materials. The tag transmits information to the PC, which is further integrated with the health care facility's information management system. On a suitable display, the doctor can view the patient's name, previously administered medications, plus recently collected vital data, such as heart rate, body temperature, and blood pressure. Without disturbing the sleeping patient or having to make further checks at a nursing station, the doctor has received all the accurate, up-to-date information she needs.

This imagery may represent a hypothetical story, but it is also a factual example. Jacobi Medical Center in the Bronx, New York has installed such a system using equipment provided by Siemens. Chief Information Officer Daniel Morreale reports: "We get 100% accuracy in identifying patients and an overall savings of clinician time because doctors and nurses get the patient information they need at the beside. This enhances patient care, supports our safety goals, and enhances the patient's experience by limiting disturbances" (*Business Week,* Special Advertising Section, February 14, 2005).

ROADMAP TO THE FUTURE

The ability to work from anywhere in the world is no longer a dream. It is a defining feature of contemporary business. By extending access to enterprise applications, employees can now use what otherwise would be lost time to develop further improvements. The ability to work in short intervals away from the normal office also frees up users to participate in revenue-generating projects. Missing deadlines or failing to secure vital information become less frequent occurrences. Collaborating with supply chain partners is made easier. Quite simply, workers have found that personal digital assistants and handheld communicators are quite powerful and business friendly. Convenient access to information has become a way of business life. RFID enhances that life.

CONCLUSIONS

Throughout this text, we have tried to pay attention to the advocates and cynics supporting or resisting acceptance of RFID technology in supply chains and elsewhere in our daily lives. Arguments for and against adoption have been presented. Our position should be clear, as we stand with the advocates and suggest that any business engaged in supply chain processing should begin work on some sort of controlled pilot operation to test and validate the opportunities and advantages of RFID deployment. Make no mistake — RFID is an inevitable technology, and finding its place in your supply chain now rather than later will pay enormous dividends. Delaying action can only forestall investments that must be accepted.

Start by creating greater visibility within the supply chain processing, tracking movements across important process steps, and expand to discovering the factual improvements that can result from knowing exactly where products and artifacts are within the extended enterprise at work delivering satisfaction to the eventual users. Progress to establishing a wireless environment, in which mobility brings a new dimension to performance and customer satisfaction. Then expand your mind to determine just how far reaching the impacts of having greater access to real-time information can be to a business. Above all, keep an open mind regarding just how far a wireless environment can expand and how you and your firm will participate in such a world.

APPENDIX

A SUMMARY OF RFID STANDARDS*

It's commonly said that there are no standards in RFID. In fact, there are many well-established standards and a few emerging standards. Here's a guide to the most important ones.

Standards are critical for many RFID applications, such as payment systems and tracking goods or reusable containers in open supply chains. A great deal of work has been going on over the past decade to develop standards for different RFID frequencies and applications.

There are existing and proposed RFID standards that deal with the air interface protocol (the way tags and readers communicate), data content (the way data is organized or formatted), conformance (ways to test that products meet the standard) and applications (how standards are used on shipping labels, for example).

The International Organization for Standardization (ISO) has created standards for tracking cattle with RFID. ISO 11784 defines how data is structured on the tag. ISO 11785 defines the air interface protocol. ISO has created a standard for the air interface protocol for RFID tags used in payment systems and contactless smart cards (ISO 14443) and in vicinity cards (ISO 15693). It also has established standards for testing the conformance of RFID tags and readers to a standard (ISO 18047), and for testing the performance of RFID tags and readers (ISO 18046).

Using RFID to track goods in open supply chains is relatively new and fewer standards have been finalized. ISO has proposed standards for tracking 40-foot shipping containers, pallets, transport units, cases and unique items. These are at various stages in the approval process.

The standard situation was complicated by the fact that the Auto-ID Center, which developed Electronic Product Code technologies, chose to create its own air interface protocol for tracking goods through the international supply chain. This article explains the evolution of the Electronic Product Code and the importance of various ISO standards.

The Auto-ID Center was set up in 1999 to develop the Electronic Product Code and related technologies that could be used to identify products and track them through the global supply chain. Its mission was to develop a low-cost RFID system, because the tags needed to be disposable (a manufacturer putting tags on products shipped to a retailer was never going to get those tags back to reuse them). It had to operate in the ultra-high frequency band, because only UHF delivered the read range needed for supply chain applications, such as reading pallets coming through a dock door.

The Auto-ID Center also wanted its RFID system to be global and to be based on open standards. It needed to be global because the aim was to use it to track goods as they flowed from a manufacturer in one country or region to companies in other regions and eventually to store shelves. For Company A to read a tag put on a product by Company B, the tag had to use a standardized air interface protocol. The Auto-ID Center developed its own protocol and licensed it to EPCglobal on the condition that it would be made available royalty-free to manufacturers and end users.

The center also was charged with developing a network architecture — a layer integrated with the Internet — that would enable anyone to look up information associated with a serial number stored on a tag. The network, too, needed to be based on open standards used on the Internet, so companies could share information easily and at low cost.

One option the Auto-ID Center had was to develop the numbering system and network infrastructure and use ISO protocols as the standard for the air interface. Earlier, EAN International and the Uniform Code Council had merged their efforts to create the Global Tag (GTAG), with ISO's UHF protocol. But the Auto-ID Center rejected this, because the ISO UHF protocol was too complex and would increase the cost of the tag unnecessarily.

The Auto-ID Center developed its own UHF protocol. Originally, the center planned to have one protocol that could be used to communicate with different classes of tags. Each successive class of tags would be more sophisticated than the one below it. The classes changed over time, but here is what was originally proposed.

- Class 1: a simple, passive, read-only backscatter tag with one-time, field-programmable non-volatile memory.
- Class 2: a passive backscatter tag with up to 65 KB of read-write memory.
- Class 3: a semi-passive backscatter tag, with up to 65 KB read-write memory; essentially, a Class 2 tag with a built-in battery to support increased read range.
- Class 4: an active tag that uses a built-in battery to run the microchip's circuitry and to power a transmitter that broadcasts a signal to a reader.
- Class 5: an active RFID tag that can communicate with other Class 5 tags and/or other devices.

Eventually, the Auto-ID Center adopted a Class 0 tag, which was a read-only tag that was programmed at the time the microchip was made. The Class 0 tag used a different protocol from the Class 1 tag, which meant that end users had to buy multiprotocol readers to read both Class 1 and Class 0 tags.

In 2003, the Auto-ID Center transitioned into two separate organizations. Auto-ID Labs at MIT and other universities around the world continued primary research on EPC technologies. EPC technology was licensed to the Uniform Code Council, which set up EPCglobal as a joint venture with EAN International, to commercialize EPC technology. In September 2003, the Auto-ID Center handed off the Class 0 and Class 1 protocols to EPCglobal, and EPCglobal's board subsequently approved Class 0 and Class 1 as EPC standards.

Class 1 and Class 0 have a couple of shortcomings, in addition to the fact that they are not interoperable. One issue is that they are incompatible with ISO standards. EPCglobal could submit them to ISO for approval as an international standard, but it is likely that ISO would want to revise them to bring them into line with ISO RFID standards. Another issue is that they cannot be used globally. Class 0, for instance, sends out a signal at one frequency and receives a signal back at a different frequency within the UHF band; this is prohibited in Europe, according to some experts (European Union regulations are open to interpretation).

In 2004, EPCglobal began developing a second-generation protocol (Gen 2), which would not be backward compatible with either Class 1 or Class 0. The aim was to create a single, global standard that would be more closely aligned with ISO standards. Gen 2 was approved in December 2004. RFID vendors that had worked on the ISO UHF standard also worked on Gen 2.

Gen 2 was designed to be fast-tracked within ISO, but a last minute disagreement over something called an Application Family Identifier (AFI) is likely to slow ISO approval. All ISO RFID standards have an AFI, an 8-bit code that identifies the origin of the data on the tag. Gen 2 has an 8-bit block of code that can be used for an AFI, but it is not required under the standard. (Requiring the eight bits to be used for an ISO AFI would have limited EPCglobal's control over EPCs.) But vendors are making product based on the new Gen 2 standard, which paves the way for global adoption of EPC technology in the supply chain.

ISO STANDARDS

ISO has developed RFID standards for automatic identification and item management. This standard, known as the ISO 18000 series, covers the air interface protocol for systems likely to be used to track goods in the supply chain. They cover the major frequencies used in RFID systems around the world. The seven parts are:

18000-1: Generic parameters for air interfaces for globally accepted frequencies
18000-2: Air interface for 135 kHz
18000-3: Air interface for 13.56 MHz
18000-4: Air interface for 2.45 GHz
18000-5: Air interface for 5.8 GHz
18000-6: Air interface for 860 MHz to 930 MHz
18000-7: Air interface at 433.92 MHz

EPCglobal's Gen 2 standard could be submitted to ISO under 18000-6, but it's not clear when that will happen or how quickly it will be approved. ISO slowed approval of 18000-6 to see if it could be aligned with Gen 2. EPCglobal has set up a committee to try to resolve the issue. Requiring an AFI would require going through a formal process of amending the EPC standard. End users would like there to be one international standard for tracking goods through the open supply chain using UHF RFID tags. But it could take another year before that finally happens.

PARTNERING DIAGNOSTIC LABORATORY

A partnering diagnostic lab (PDL) is a facilitated exercise involving multiple supply chain constituents determined to find a higher level of collaboration and results from a focus on existing conditions and potential process improvements. The PDL develops mutually beneficial improvements through an examination of all aspects of a business relationship in an area targeted for improvement.

It could encompass technical, transactional, procurement, and logistics activities or product, information, and cash flow considerations. A typical PDL includes an intensive search for:

■ New methods and procedures that positively alter process steps in normal business activities between two or more companies
■ Finding hidden values across the involved supply chain network processes connecting the participants
■ New processes and features of electronic commerce that improve quality and shorten cycle times
■ A roadmap toward optimized conditions in an extended enterprise that introduces cost reductions and better use of assets and builds greater customer satisfaction and new revenues

As seen in Figure A.1, a PDL is a focused, facilitated, fact-supported two-day session convened between two or more businesses to resolve how to improve intercompany supply chain processes and establish win-win solutions to help both entities increase performance. The secret to a successful PDL is to invite a larger cross-section of individuals than would normally be involved in intercompany discussions to participate in analyzing current process steps to discover innovative solutions to root causes. These participants could include

• **What it is**
 – A *focused, facilitated, fact-supported* 2-day session between businesses to **resolve** how to improve intercompany supply chain processes

• **Who participates**
 – Appropriate representatives from both companies, e.g.
  • Supplier: Sales/Marketing, IT, R&D
  • Customer: Purchasing, Manufacturing, Planning, IT, R&D

• **When it is held**
 – After preliminary discussions with both parties to:
  • Identify opportunity areas
  • Define specific processes for improvement
  • Gather supporting data

• **Where it is held**
 – At the sponsor's offices or plant or selected off-site facility

Figure A.1.   PDL Overview

sales and marketing, information technology, and research and development from a supplier and purchasing, manufacturing, planning, IT, and R&D from a customer. The idea is to broaden the scope of who attends so people normally kept from conversations have a chance to voice an active opinion on how a situation can be enhanced. Specific opportunities for action are defined through the chartering of improvement teams and performance measures to track benefits from changed processing.

A preliminary discussion with the parties to be involved, to develop a current-situation assessment, identify potential areas of opportunity, and define specific processes for attention and gathering of supporting data, is held at a selected site. During this necessary prediagnostic discussion, the objective is to explain the procedure and develop ideas and concepts to be considered in the PDL and to agree on the framework for the discussion. Activities could include such areas as:

- Development of a process map to describe the area under consideration
- Consideration of best practices that could have a positive impact on the processing
- Development of ideas to achieve extra values, through:
  - □ Reduced cycle times for process completion
  - □ Aggregated purchasing
  - □ Reduced dependency on inventory and safety stocks (raw materials, work in process, and finished goods)
  - □ Enhanced communication between parties, especially Internet-based linkage to improve service features
  - □ Better utilization of joint assets
  - □ Aggregated transportation opportunities
  - □ Increased online visibility to supply chain process steps

One necessary outcome of the preliminary meetings is to determine the scope, purpose, details, and deliverables from the work sessions. Another is to specify the attendees for the PDL, making certain there are face-to-face conditions for people from both participants (i.e., IT people who are involved from both the supplying and buying perspectives, delivery and receiving personnel). Through interviews with appropriate executives and possible attendees, a situation assessment is created to describe the as-is conditions and to serve as a starting point for the eventual discussion. A list of preliminary ideas for discussion will be generated, an outline of the scope and details of the working sessions accepted, and a sample letter of invitation prepared with the proposed agenda for the PDL.

Following the preliminary discussion and interviews, a site is selected, attendees are invited, and the two-day PDL session is conducted. During this session, open and frank discussions are encouraged. Each attendee is given an opportunity to express views and to present at least one expected deliverable for attending and participating. The process map, from the perspectives of the two or more firms represented, is discussed and agreement reached on the as-is conditions. Following a consideration of current best practices in similar areas of processing, the facilitator moves the discussion to how the process map can be improved. After what generally results in 30 to 50 possible improvement ideas, the suggestions are placed in categories and breakout teams are dispatched to develop specific suggestions for changes and enhancements. A final prioritized list of improvement opportunities is generated.

The final phase is to prepare specific action plans for at least five to ten of the highest potential ideas, including team sponsor, scope of the action, required resources, action steps, timetable for completion, and order-of-magnitude costs and benefits. These actions are placed on an action grid, complete with priority ranking and timing of execution. Typical benefits achieved range from 5 to 20 percent of the costs involved, depending on the length of the relationship, the depth of current obstacles and problems, closeness of the relationship, and previous continuous improvement initiatives. Figure A.2 depicts the generalized approach involved in a PDL.

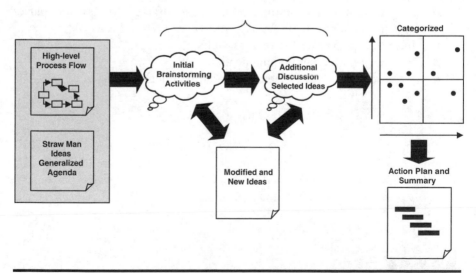

Figure A.2.   Generalized Approach for Two-Day PDL Workshop

Potential benefits are extensive. Based on many PDLs, they could include:

- Reduced errors in order processing
- Savings in order fulfillment costs
  - ☐ Order to delivery
  - ☐ Order to cash
- Lower inventory
- Less warehouse space
- Reduced freight costs
- New customer-centric metrics that drive enhanced performance
- Higher customer satisfaction ratings
- E-commerce interconnectivity features
- Communications enhancements
- New, profitable revenues

Intangible benefits derive as well, including:

- Better understanding of supply chain concepts and strategies
- Better understanding of operational aspects of the particular supply chain process steps
- Strengthened customer/supplier relationships
- Product rationalization
- Improved design for manufacture
- Alignment of manufacturing and materials strategies with marketplace-driven realities
- Increased partnering between IT units
- Enhanced partnering communication
- Increased knowledge of processes and applications

BIBLIOGRAPHY

Alvarez, Gene, "RFID Helps Enterprises Increase Return on Assets Through Tracking," *Information Week RFID Insights,* December 21, 2004.

Bacheldor, Beth, "Suppliers Sign On as GE Powers Up RFID Effort," *Information Week,* October 27, 2003a, p. 28.

Bacheldor, Beth, "Luggage Tag Has a Whole New Meaning," *Information Week,* November 10, 2003b, p. 32.

Balfour, Frederick, "Fakes!" *Business Week,* February 7, 2005, pp. 54–64.

Boyle, Matthew, "Wal-Mart Keeps the Change," *Fortune,* November 10, 2003, p. 46.

Buss, Dale, "Signal Achievements in the Supply Chain," *Automotive Logistics,* May/June 2004, pp. 68–71.

Byrnes, Jonathan, "Who Will Profit from Auto-ID?" *Harvard Business School Working Knowledge,* September 1, 2003.

Chabrow, Eric, "Homeland Security Unveils US-Visit Details," www.informationweek.com, October 28, 2003.

Chabrow, Eric, "Homeland Security to Test RFID Tags at U.S. Borders," www.informationweek.com, January 25, 2005a.

Chabrow, Eric, "Homeland Security to Test RFID at Borders," *Information Week,* January 31, 2005b, p. 26.

Collins, Jonathan, "Hitachi Unveils Integrated RFID Tag," *RFID Journal,* September 4, 2003.

Connolly, Allison, "Military Pushing Switch from Bar Codes to RFID Tags for Shipping," www.manufacturing.net, January 31, 2005.

Delaney, Kevin, "Beyond Bar Code: Radio ID Tags May Soon Be Placed in Every Product Imaginable," *Wall Street Journal,* September 23, 2002.

Edwards, John, "Tag, You're It," *CIO Magazine,* February 15, 2003.

EPCglobal Network, "Overview of Design," *Benefits & Security,* September 24, 2004.

Ewalt, David M., "Navy Puts RFID into Service," *Information Week,* June 9, 2003, p. 57.

Foster, Thomas A., "On the Rebound: New Interest in Where Supply Chain Technology Can Take a Company," *Global Logistics & Supply Chain Strategies,* March 2004, pp. 32–41.

Gadh, Rajit, "Getting from Mandates to a Wireless Internet of Things," *Computerworld,* October 4, 2004.

Gartner, W. David, "Wal-Mart's RFID Suppliers Are Resisting," www.informationweek.com, December 21, 2004.

Garvey, Martin, "RFID's First Hurdle: Bar Codes," *Information Week,* March 30, 2004.

Gooley, Toby, "C-TPAT Benefits Outweigh Costs," *Supply Chain Management Review,* January/February 2005, pp. 11–12.

Hayes, Mary, "In Sync," *Information Week,* June 16, 2003, pp. 30–34.

Hulme, George, "Jenny Craig Simplifies Security," www.informationweek.com, January 26, 2005a.

Hulme, George, "RFID Helps Track Cargo Containers," www.informationweek.com, April 6, 2005b.

Intel Corporation, "Building the Digital Supply Chain: An Intel Perspective," White Paper, January 2005.

Jacques, Robert, "RFID Set for Growth Explosion," www.vnunet.com, February 28, 2005.

Kekre, Sunder, "Forging New Links for a 21st Century Supply Network," www.tepper.cmu.edu, Fall 2004.

Khermouch, Gerry and Green, Heather, "Bar Codes Better Watch Their Backs," *Business Week,* July 14, 2003, p. 42.

Kontzer, Tony, "Getting RFID into the Skies, www.informationweek.com, June 10, 2004.

Macmillan-Davies, Clive, "The Application of Radio Frequency Identification (RFID) Tags in the Australian Defence Force (ADF)," Land Warfare Conference, Adelaide, October 2003, pp. 1–13.

McGee, Marianne, "Wireless Future: Tracking Patients and Equipment," *Information Week,* May 19, 2003, p. 48.

McGee, Marianne Kolbasuk, "Drug Industry to Shift to Digital Orders," *Information Week,* January 24, 2005, p. 26.

McKinney, Joe, "Attack Invoice Deductions Through RFID," *RFID News and Solutions,* January 2005, pp. 29–30.

Purdum, Traci, "Factory to Foxhole: RFID Deadline Looms," www.industryweek.com, November 1, 2004.

Quinn, Francis, "Ready for the Auto-ID Revolution: An Interview with Kevin Ashton," *Supply Chain Management Review,* May 2003.

Ricadela, Aaron, "Sensors Everywhere," *Information Week,* January 24, 2005, pp. 33–36.

Rinehart, Lloyd, Myers, Matthew, and Eckert, James, "Supplier Relationships: The Impact on Security," *Supply Chain Management Review,* September 2004, pp. 52–59.

Roberti, Mark, Comments made at CSC RFID Exchange, Rosemont, Illinois, February 24, 2005a.

Roberti, Mark, "Purdue Pharma Gets Down to the Item," *RFID Journal,* January/February 2005b, pp. 13–21.

Roberti, Mark, "Economic Inefficiency," *RFID Journal,* January/February 2005c, p. 10.

Sarma, Sanjay, "Reading RFID," *MIT Center for Transportation & Logistics Newsletter and Calendar,* January 4, 2005, pp. 1–3.

Stockman, Harry, "Communication by Means of Reflected Power," Proceedings of the IRE, October 1948, pp. 1196–1204.

Sullivan, Laurie, "Reaching Down the Supply Chain," *Information Week,* March 22, 2004a, pp. 49–52.

Sullivan, Laurie, "Cattlemen's Beef Association Readies RFID Program," www.informationweek.com, December 23, 2004b.

Sullivan, Laurie, "RFID: The Plot Thickens," *Information Week,* January 3, 2005a, pp. 24–26.

Sullivan, Laurie, "RFID Lets NASA Monitor Hazardous Waste," www.informationweek.com, January 10, 2005b.

Sullivan, Laurie, "U.K. Retailer Goes on RFID Shopping Spree," *Information Week,* January 17, 2005c, p. 36.

Sullivan, Laurie, "Stores Win Using Analytics," *Information Week,* January 17, 2005d, p. 67.

Sullivan, Laurie, "European Retailers Accelerate RFID Plans," *Information Week,* January 24, 2005e, p. 30.

Sullivan, Laurie, "Court Puts RFID on the Docket," *Information Week,* January 31, 2005f, p. 51.

Sullivan, Laurie, "Europe Tries on RFID," *Information Week,* March 7, 2005g.

Violino, Bob, "RFID Opportunities and Challenges," *RFID Journal,* August 31, 2003.

Violino, Bob, "I Want You to Tag Your Shipments," *RFID Journal,* January/February 2005, pp. 31–35.

Zebra Technologies, "Brand Protection in the Supply Chain," Application White Paper, Vernon Hills, Illinois, 2003.

Zebra Technologies, "Track and Trace Solutions for the Life Sciences Supply Chain," Application White Paper, Vernon Hills, Illinois, 2004.

Zrimsek, Brian, "Gartner RFID Pessimism and Act-on-Fact," www.computerweekly.com, November 25, 2004.

INDEX